Amazon FBA Mastery

Your 5-Days

Beginner To Expert Guide In

Selling Highly Profitable Private

Label Products On

Amazon

By

Michael Ezeanaka

www.MichaelEzeanaka.com

Copyright ©2019

Disclaimer

This publication is designed to provide competent and reliable information regarding the subject matter covered. However, it is sold with the understanding that the author is not engaged in rendering investment or other professional advice. Laws and practices often vary from state to state and country to country and if investment or other expert assistance is required, the services of a professional should be sought. The author specifically disclaims any liability that is incurred from the use or application of the contents of this book.

Financial Freedom Mastermind

We run occasional promotions on Amazon where we discount the price of our books. If you want to join an exclusive group of people that get notified when this is about to take place, subscribe to our mailing list by going to:

www.MichaelEzeanaka.com > Financial Freedom Mastermind

Books In The Business & Money Series

Dropshipping

Affiliate Marketing

Passive Income Ideas

Facebook Advertising

Real Estate Investing For Beginners

Credit Cards And Credit Repair Secrets

Passive Income With Affiliate Marketing (2nd Edition)

The Simple Stock Market Investing Blueprint (2-in-1 Bundle)

Real Estate Investing And Credit Repair Strategies (2-in-1 Bundle)

Real Estate And Stock Market Investing Mastery (3-in-1 Bundle)

Affiliate Marketing + Passive Income Ideas (2-in-1 Bundle)

Dropshipping + Facebook Advertising (2-in-1 Bundle)

Passive Income With Dividend Investing

Stock Market Investing For Beginners

Bonus Offer

The kindle edition will be available to you for FREE when you purchase the paperback version from

Amazon.com (The US Store)

Download The Audio Versions Along With The Complementary PDF Document For FREE from

www.MichaelEzeanaka.com > My Audiobooks

Table of Contents

Introduction 6

Chapter 1 7

  Amazon FBA Business Model Explained 8

    How The Business Model Works.. 8

    As an FBA seller, you still have to: 9

    What are the benefits of Amazon FBA? 10

    What are the disadvantages of Amazon FBA? 14

    Private label business model and other ways of selling on Amazon 16

    Pros and cons of private label vs. other ways of selling on Amazon 19

    Who are the stakeholders in the private label business model? 20

Chapter 2 26

  Getting Started 26

    Steps on how to start private label selling via Amazon FBA 26

    How to create an Amazon seller central account 29

    What tools are required? 31

    What are the costs involved in selling via Amazon FBA? 34

Chapter 3 40

  Product Research 40

    Criteria for selecting a good product... 40

    Five best selling categories on Amazon 44

Chapter 4 49

  Sourcing the Product 49

    Where can you find suppliers?... 49

    How to evaluate reliability of suppliers 51

    Criteria to use when evaluating a supplier 53

    How To Spot Shady Suppliers 54

    Ordering samples... 55

Chapter 5 59

  Shipping the Products 59

    Shipping from China to Amazon Warehouse 59

    Shipping by sea or air.. 60

    Import duty of products and other taxes...................................... 64

Chapter 6 67

  Preparing the Product for Sale by Branding 67

    Building a brand that is sustainable 67

    What you need to know about trademarks 68

Chapter 7 .... **74**

  Product Launch **74**

    Reasons for doing a product launch 74

    How to do a successful product launch? 75

    Choosing the right photographer for your product 78

    Optimizing product listings to boost sales 80

    Anatomy of a product listing 82

    Amazon Advertising (AA) 83

    Testing different price points 83

Chapter 8 .... **85**

  What Comes Next? **85**

    Analyze post-launch feedbacks 85

    Improve the product 86

    Create new products 87

    Add complementary products 87

Chapter 9 .... **92**

  Scaling $10,000 a Month and Beyond **92**

Conclusion **97**

Book(s) By Michael Ezeanaka **98**

Introduction

Today, millions of people all over the world do their shopping online. And one great thing that came out of this whole internet shopping phenomenon is the opportunity given to individual sellers to compete on equal footing against big companies and retailers. Setting up an e-commerce business is not as costly as opening a physical store that requires you to pay for monthly rent, utilities, and so on. You can set up shop in your basement and run your business behind the computer in the comforts of your home.

One of the most popular e-commerce websites and online retailers is Amazon. In fact, according to one study, Amazon is the starting point of 44% of online shoppers, with Google trailing behind at 33%. Moreover, 40% of people who live in the United States buy at least one item every month from the website. No wonder it has become the central hub of online buying and selling.

And if you are specifically thinking of selling your own stuff with your own private label on Amazon, and have them take care of storage and fulfillment to customers, you have come to the right place because this book will teach you everything you need to know about Amazon FBA, which is exactly what you need. Combine your hard work and business acumen with high quality products and Amazon FBA, and you will surely be well on your way to great success.

Without further ado, let's get right into it!

Helpful Resource - Fiverr

Fiverr is just the right platform that an employer on the hunt for a freelancer needs. You can find just about any product or service you need – *all starting at $5*. The platform works by having freelancers post their services and work samples. Buyers simply have to look up the best one that would suit their needs. Common services include logo design, contract writing and even hiring a virtual assistant.

To Learn More, go to **www.MichaelEzeanaka.com > Resources > Fiverr**

Chapter 1

Amazon FBA Business Model Explained

Before you get too excited and start sending all your products to Amazon, you should first understand what the Amazon FBA business model is all about. Amazon FBA literally stands for Fulfilled by Amazon and it gives third-party vendors access to Amazon's facilities and services. Launched in 2016, Amazon FBA is just one of the different business models that Amazon offers to its partner sellers. If you register to this program, you are taking advantage of Amazon's huge facilities, efficient cataloguing, advanced shipping, and customer service. How cool is that?

Amazon gets half of its sales from third party vendors like you, and 66% of the top 10,000 Amazon vendors use FBA.

How The Business Model Works

You send all your products, whether used or brand new, to one of Amazon's fulfillment centers. These are huge warehouses where they store all the products sent by sellers like you. These fulfillment centers are massive, the largest covers an area of 1,264,200 square feet and is located in Texas. The warehouses are run not only by employees but also by robots. As of 2018, they have 75 fulfillment centers across North America. Add to this the additional 25 sortation centers, where items are sorted to be delivered to different locations, and you get an idea how Amazon can handle such a huge undertaking.

When your products reach one of these fulfillment centers, they will then be sorted and catalogued. You do not have to worry about your products getting lost or damaged in these huge warehouses because they are well taken care of by employees and robots, and everything is computerized. And on the off-chance (which means it is an extremely rare occurrence) that one of your products gets damaged while in the fulfillment centers, you can consider it sold because Amazon will pay for the full retail price of the item.

Now you just wait for someone to buy your item listed on the Amazon website. Amazon will handle the whole transaction when a customer buys your listed product on the website. The whole process is automated, which makes it a lot faster.

Since the items in the warehouse are assigned their unique inventory code, it is easier to find them among the hundreds of shelves lined up inside the huge warehouse. The item will be packaged and delivered to the buyer by Amazon on your behalf.

Once the item is delivered to the customer, Amazon will follow up to ensure that there are no problems with the shipment and that the customer is satisfied with the order. Amazon also handles customer service for FBA items, and also returns and refunds, with your assistance of course.

So what are your responsibilities as a seller? You still have something to do, right? Of course, you do. Amazon FBA just shoulders half of the work so that you can focus your attention and efforts on other things that are also important when managing an e-commerce business.

As an FBA seller, you still have to:

1. Determine the products that you want to sell.

Amazon will not help you choose what products you want to sell, and they also will not source your products for you. You still have to do your research on what products sell well, and where you can source them. You also have to know how much the products are going for online and in physical stores so that you can have a rough estimate on how much profit you will be getting. One important tip to remember is to sell fast-moving items because you have to pay for their storage in the fulfillment center.

2. Monitor your inventory levels.

It is your responsibility as a seller to check if you still have enough products to sell that are in storage. Since these items are in the fulfillment centers, it is easy to lose track of how much you still have because you cannot see them in person, unlike when you keep your stocks in your own place. Although Amazon will let you know if your inventory is running low, it is still up to you to be proactive and ensure that you have enough products to sell.

3. Market and promote your products.

This does not mean you have to pay expensive TV or print ads. Maybe that's how it was many years ago. Online advertising is different. It is a lot less expensive and you need to use the right techniques more than money. If you are a re-seller of brand name products that are already highly-ranked, you may no longer need to do this step because the big corporations already have their own million-dollar ads and billboards. But if you are selling your own custom products or private label products, then you have to do this step and make sure that people can see your products. Remember that Amazon has millions of products listed online, which makes marketing an essential step if you want people to find your items for sale.

What are the benefits of Amazon FBA?

Based on what you have read so far, you probably get an idea about the kinds of benefits that you will get if you decide to sell your own private label products using Amazon FBA. But to give you a clearer view of the different benefits of Amazon FBA that can help you decide if it is something that you want to try, continue reading the next points.

1. Efficient logistics, cheaper shipping rates, and faster delivery time

If you are selling a few products, it is easier to handle everything on your own and in your own house. You do not really need to rent a place for storage or to hire people. But if you are thinking of starting an e-commerce business as a main source of income, and you are going to sell a lot of products, then you need a more efficient way to handle and ship all your items on time. And hiring professionals to do all these things for you may be expensive. With Amazon, you are taking advantage of their expertise and experience with shipping and logistics. After all, they are the biggest e-commerce website in the world right now, and being efficient goes with the territory.

Moreover, when shipping items, you have to consider different rules and regulations. Different factors affect shipping fees such as the weight and size of the product, the kind of product you are going to ship, and so on. You also need to research about international shipping (in case you decide to make your products available to international buyers), areas served by the courier, prohibited and restricted commodities, insurance, and so many things. If you use Amazon FBA, you do not have to worry because Amazon will take care of these things for you.

Third party sellers like yourself and online shoppers both benefit from this because the entire shipping process is a lot faster. After all, your items are already in their warehouses and they have partnerships with big courier companies because they ship thousands, if not millions, of items worldwide. Amazon also has fulfillment centers all over the world, which allows them to deliver customer orders within just a couple of days. This is because when a customer buys a product from you, they do not necessarily get the exact item that you sent to Amazon. Amazon sort like products together, so if a customer buys a specific item, say, a Mickey Mouse t-shirt, and you live in the United States and your buyer lives in Canada, they will search for a similar item in the fulfillment center closest to the buyer, which significantly shortens the delivery period and also makes shipping fee a lot cheaper.

Shipping is also generally cheaper if you let Amazon handle it for you because, as I mentioned previously, they have partnerships with big shipping companies and they can get discounts because they ship a lot of items (i.e. economy of scale). And to attract higher sales, Amazon passes on this incentive to the sellers and buyers. You, as a seller, can get reduced shipping costs when sending your products to one of their fulfillment centers. And FBA products are often eligible for free shipping, especially to buyers who are Amazon Prime members. It boosts Amazon's sales, attracts more buyers for you, and saves customers on shipping costs. It is a win-win-win type of situation for all parties involved.

2. More free time for you

Managing an e-commerce business can be time-consuming especially if you handle everything by yourself — from sourcing products to sell, taking pictures, storing, packaging, pricing, shipping, and handling customer service. If you leverage the Amazon FBA business model, you are freeing up a lot of your time that you can use to concentrate on more important things such as choosing products for your online store, sourcing the products, and taking great photos. And the more time you spend on these things, the higher quality of products and the better photos you will have in your online store. And besides, these are the fun parts of selling products online.

Shopping for things to resell or making them yourself is what makes people do online selling. A lot of sellers also enjoy photography so taking pictures of their products is just like a hobby for most of them. The boring parts of managing an e-commerce business are the shipping and logistics, and also handling returns and customer complaints. And thankfully, this can all be taken care of by Amazon through FBA.

You can use your free time to research on what products to sell, how to improve your products, how to promote your products, the current prices of similar products on the market, and how to scale up your business. You can also focus on taking great pictures of your items for sale. Remember that in online selling, pictures paint a thousand words, and it is sometimes what makes or breaks a sale. If your picture does not look good, some people will question the quality of your product and will not buy them, no matter how great your product actually is.

Aside from spending your free time doing things to grow your business, you can also use it for doing personal stuff, such as travelling, spending time with your loved ones, learning a new hobby, and so on. It gives you the perfect balance between your business and your personal life. Some people even continue working their regular full-time job while managing their e-commerce business.

3. Huge storage space

You can live in a tiny house and still sell huge products without the need for a large storage space if you are using Amazon FBA because all of your stuff will be stored in their humongous fulfillment centers. Not having enough storage space at home sometimes stops a lot of people from selling big items or keeping a large inventory. Your house or even a rented commercial space can only hold a limited amount of stuff.

You do not have to worry about boxes and packages cluttered in your living room or bedroom because Amazon takes care of all this. Having boxes and packages that you need to step over inside your house can be hazardous and can cause accidents. You do not want this to happen at all. And renting your own warehouse can be costly, especially if you are just starting because apart from the monthly rent, you have to pay for utilities such as electricity, internet connection, and even water in some instances.

Another good thing about sending your stuff to Amazon is that there is no minimum inventory required. Heck, you can even send just one product if you really do not have any storage at all in your house. Amazon also gives an incentive to sellers whose products move fast, meaning they don't stay for a long time in the storage facility. You can get unlimited storage if your items sell like hotcakes, so to speak.

Moreover, Amazon fulfillment centers have the right kind of storage for certain products. For instance, if you are selling leather bags or shoes, you do not want to store them in your basement where the high humidity and temperature can cause damage to your products.

4. Amazon's good reputation

It is not hard to believe that Amazon is the leading online selling platform because it is reliable, and a lot of buyers and sellers trust its business platform. If you use Amazon FBA, you are also benefiting from Amazon's strong reputation. They have already established their brand name and collaborating with them will do your business a lot of good. For people who are just starting to sell online, selling products through Amazon will bring them higher sales than selling their products through their own website.

Although there is nothing wrong with having your own website, it poses a bigger risk for individual sellers than if they bring their business to a well-known selling platform that already has an established reputation, such as Amazon. And it is even better if you use Amazon FBA because buyers would know that a large company is handling certain aspects of your business for you.

As you establish your own brand and reputation, you can maybe then focus solely on selling on your very own website. But for now, Amazon is the easiest way to get higher sales. In fact, even established companies and sellers still use Amazon as an online selling platform because they know that they will get a higher reach since millions of people are now using Amazon.

5. Handles customer service and returns

This is another one of the less attractive features of having your own business—handling customer service and returns. Before buying a product, some customers already have a lot of question. And this is handled by people who work at Amazon. They have customer service centers that provide support 24/7 through phone calls, emails, and chat. If they have more questions or even complaints upon receiving the item, Amazon will also take care of it for you. This is a really great benefit, especially for people who love the whole mechanics of selling online, but not the part where you have to talk to the customer.

In fact, a lot of people prefer online selling over the traditional form of selling where you have to talk to the person face to face because they are not comfortable at this kind of set up. This is why having someone else do this for you is a great help. Moreover, Amazon customer service representatives are trained to handle different concerns and complaints. They can handle even the most irate customers because that's what they are trained to do.

Another thing that they handle for you is returns. Handling returns can be a hassle because you not only have to deal with upset customers but also the logistics and administrative aspect of having the product returned to you and the payment returned to the customer. They also have to do inspection to check if the item is really damaged before shipping it to the customer or not. All of this is handled by Amazon. Of course, there is a corresponding fee but it is worth the small amount that you have to pay for the work and trouble that they take off your plate.

6. Increase your sales

Ultimately, this is the main goal of all this, why you are selling online and why you are partnering with Amazon. You want to make sure that you have high sales even on a website like Amazon, where you will surely have a lot of competitors. All the benefits that you can enjoy using Amazon FBA boil down to this — attracting more buyers and boosting your sales. You may think that you are getting less because you have to pay Amazon different kinds of fees, but the efficiency and expertise allow you to sell more items at a quicker rate, which means higher sales for you in a shorter period of time. Besides, the fees are worth it because you are using their top-of-the-line facilities and expertise in online selling. You are even saving money because you do not have to pay for your own warehouse and hire staff or assistants who will help you with all of these once your business starts to grow.

What are the disadvantages of Amazon FBA?

Just like with all kinds of business models, Amazon FBA also has disadvantages, although it is already an incredible online selling platform. After all, no business model is perfect. You also need to understand the different disadvantages of Amazon FBA before you decide to use it in your e-commerce business.

1. Amazon FBA costs money

Not everything in life is free, and if you expect to get top notch service and expertise, then you should be willing to pay the price. This is also true if you decide to use Amazon FBA. You have to pay for the storage of your products. The longer your products stay in their fulfillment centers, the more you have to pay. This is why it is important to ensure that your products sell quickly. Do not let them stay in Amazon storage for more than six months.

Be prepared to pay sky-high storage fees if your inventory sits for a long time. Because of this, you have to take this into consideration. Will you still make a profit even after all the storage fees that you paid for that particular item? Although you can sell large items, you have to make sure that they will move fast because this can cost you a lot in terms of storage. It is also not ideal to store cheap items where you only get a small profit in Amazon fulfillment centers because you might end up paying more for the storage than the actual product itself.

2. Monitoring inventory can be challenging

Although you can always ask Amazon about your inventory, it is still more difficult to track your inventory if you do not see them in person. It is hard to determine what products you still have, what's been sitting in storage for months, what you need to re-order, when you need to buy more, and so on. If your inventory is in plain sight, you will be able to know right away which ones are selling and which ones are not. This makes it even more challenging during the holiday season, when people buy a lot of their gifts for their loved ones online and orders come in by the thousands.

3. Co-mingling can be tricky

Amazon sorts similar items together in their fulfillment centers for efficiency. For example, Amazon will group all Adidas Stan Smith sneakers from different sellers together. This means that a person who clicked your listing and purchased the item does not necessarily mean that he will be getting the sneakers that you sent, although he will still get his Stan Smiths. You have the option to take advantage of this feature if you want to.

However, this can be scary for some because not all sellers are reliable and trustworthy. Some even send damaged or counterfeit products, and if you are unlucky and the buyer got that damaged or counterfeit item that another seller has sent, then you will be the one getting the negative feedback. Some legitimate sellers were even banned from selling on Amazon because of this, although this is a rare case.

4. Amazon controls about half of your business

When partnering with Amazon via FBA, you are giving up a lot of control over your business. For example, you cannot choose the kind of packaging that you want for your items and you cannot also add a personal touch such a short thank you note or some customized stickers and freebies into the package because Amazon handles all the packaging and shipping. You cannot tell them to use a silvery packaging paper or use eco-friendly packaging. They do things their way, which is of course more efficient but does not have the personal touch that you would want your buyers to experience when they buy items from your online shop.

5. Product prep can be difficult

You need to follow certain guidelines when sending out your inventory to Amazon. It can be time consuming and tedious, especially for beginners but you will soon get the hang of it after doing it several times. For example, there are different rules to follow for sending multiples of the same products in one package, single products, single products with different parts, and so on. You also have to use the right kind of bag for your items. There are also special instructions for sending adult products, e.g. using a shrink wrap or a black, opaque poly bag. There are so many things to consider when prepping, packaging, and labeling your products to be sent out to Amazon that there is a separate chapter only for this topic, which you will see later on.

Private label business model and other ways of selling on Amazon

This book is all about selling private label products through Amazon FBA. There are different ways to sell on Amazon, and one of them is by selling private label items.

1. Private label

As the name implies, private label means you choose a specific product to sell under your own private label or brand via Amazon FBA. If you are a private label seller, you decide on which product you want to sell, for instance clothes. You source them from a supplier, usually from China, and make them your own private label or brand. A third-party supplier under a contract manufactures the items.

To find products that you can sell under your own private label, you need to do a lot of research and studying, especially involving the market and what sells profitably and what doesn't. You are also responsible for contacting the suppliers or manufacturers. This is something that you cannot delegate to Amazon. You even have the option to have all the products shipped directly to Amazon by the third-party supplier, which means that all you need to do is to sit behind your laptop and manage your whole business.

With private label, you are not hindered by not having enough resources or skills to create the product that you want to sell because you can find a supplier who will do all of these for you. For example, if you want to sell clothes under your own logo or label, you do not really need to be a seamstress or buy all the materials needed for making clothes because all you need to do is to find someone who can do this for you. You can order them in bulk and have the products shipped to Amazon either directly by the manufacturer or by you.

2. Retail arbitrage

This is another way to sell products on Amazon. You search for low-priced branded products online or in retail stores, and resell them on Amazon at a marked up price. Retail arbitrage sellers often go to the clearance racks of giant retail corporations such as Target, Walmart, and Home Depot for their inventory.

For example, there is a sale on school supplies in Target and you are able to purchase a pack of 12 ballpoint pens for a discounted price of $3. You buy them and resell them on Amazon for $8, which is a little lower than their regular price of $12. You still earn a profit even if you sell it at a significantly lower price compared to the regular price. You also have the choice to sell it at the regular price of $12 if you want, especially if you know that these pens are highly sought after.

Private label sellers, on the other hand, only source their products from one manufacturer. The products are also sold under their own brand name while retail arbitrage sellers keep the brand name of their products, unless they want to be sued for intellectual property theft. Retail arbitrage is what a lot of people do when they sell online, especially those who are just part-time sellers who do not have a huge budget to buy things in bulk and establish their own brand name.

3. Wholesale

Buying wholesale from manufacturers and selling them as is on Amazon at a higher price is another way of selling on Amazon. You cannot sell the products under your own name or add value to the products because you are selling products under an established brand name. For example, you can buy wholesale Sony mobile phone cases directly from Sony and sell them as Sony mobile phone cases. You cannot rename the brand and change it to your own private label or you will be sued.

It is a bit similar to private label because you buy in bulk. The main difference is that you go to a manufacturer with the intention of buying their products in bulk and reselling these products while keeping the manufacturer's own brand. With private label selling, you go to a manufacturer and you agree upon a contract that includes buying their products in bulk that suits your business requirements, adding value to these products, and selling them under your own brand.

Wholesale buying and reselling is also kind of similar to retail arbitrage because manufacturers get to keep their own brand name. The main difference is that in wholesale, you source bulk products from one manufacturer, and in retail arbitrage, you source them from many different retailers.

4. Used book sales

Selling used books via Amazon is one of the easiest ways to start an online business that does not require a lot of capital. Financial risk is much lower when you sell used books. After all, you can just sell whatever you already have at home and you can easily buy used books for just a few dollars. Moreover, selling used books will also not get you as much complaints or returns from consumers as compared to selling other types of products unless you mistakenly sent the wrong book. You can even use the money that you earn from selling used books to launch your own private label business.

Pros and cons of private label vs. other ways of selling on Amazon

Private label vs. retail arbitrage

The drawback of retail arbitrage is that you have to continuously search for items on sale at different places. With private label, you already have a contract with one supplier, unless you decide to change your supplier or add more products to sell, which makes sourcing a lot easier. Your shop will also have more variety in terms of type or brand if you do retail arbitrage whereas private label selling means fewer types of products and only one brand (your private brand) to sell.

The amount of products you can buy depends solely on your budget if you decide to do private label selling. On the other hand, the amount of products you can sell using retail arbitrage depends not only on your budget but also on the availability of the product. The pens that you were able to buy for $3 and resell for $8 may no longer be available next time there is another sale. Because of this unpredictability, it is difficult to get consistent sales with retail arbitrage. Your profit margins will be variable, depending on how much you were able to get the item for.

Going back to our pen example, you might be able to find them again the next time they are on sale, but the discounted price may not be the same. It may be higher ($5 for 12 pens) or lower ($1 for all 12!). Retail arbitrage depends a lot on chance (of stumbling upon great deals) while private label is all about careful planning. This is why selling private labeled products has a bigger potential to grow, but at the same time, the risks of losing a lot of money is also much higher, especially if you are selling a single type of product in your shop.

Private label vs. wholesale

Both methods of selling get their products in bulk from one supplier, which means that sourcing is easy for both. And since both buy products in bulk, profit margins can easily be determined because they already have an idea about the base price of the products, and how much they go for in the market.

The main difference between the two, as mentioned earlier, is the branding. When you buy wholesale from a manufacturer, you resell the products under the manufacturer's brand. When you do private label selling, you can add value to your product and sell them under your own brand. Private label selling gives you more control because you can do whatever you want with the products once you buy them from the manufacturer.

Another difference between wholesale and private label is that in wholesale, you have to find a manufacturer that is not already selling directly on Amazon. You see that a lot of these popular brands also have their own accounts on Amazon. And how can you compete with the manufacturer selling their products on the same online selling platform?

But if you really become successful in private label selling, you can turn your online business into a multimillion company. Your name will be associated with your brand, which you created all on your own. Multimillionaires did not become rich by reselling products that they buy from existing brands. They created their own brands, and source the products somewhere else. Or better yet, you can create your own product. But that is another topic for another day.

Private label vs. retail arbitrage and wholesale

Basically, you are building your own brand from scratch with private label selling, unlike wholesale and retail arbitrage. It involves a higher financial risk than the other two but the rewards are also much greater if your business becomes successful. With retail arbitrage and wholesale reselling, the products that you sell already have an established brand. You do not really need to launch or promote them because the manufacturers already have their own ads for their products on different media such as TV, radio, print, and online. All you need to do is to make sure that your shop is visible enough so that when the customers search for the products, they will see your online store on top. People already know the products and the brand that you are selling. With private selling, you have to do a launch to let people know about your brand and the kind of products that you sell. You also have to make sure that you promote your products by advertising and making your shop more visible online.

Who are the stakeholders in the private label business model?

The three main stakeholders in this kind of business model are the following: the business owner (you), the manufacturer, and Amazon. In between and under these categories, there are minor players that make up the whole business model and make things run more smoothly and efficiently. Let's discuss the major stakeholders first.

1. The business owner

This refers to you, the person who has the idea to start an online business selling niche products under his own brand. You are responsible for determining the kind of products that you can sell through Amazon or even other channels. This means that you have to spend time doing research. There are already thousands of sellers of clothes. You can still sell clothes, but you need to find a niche where no one or very few has gone before. For example, you can sell funny hats instead of normal looking hats.

Your products need to stand out from the rest if you want people to notice and buy them. As the business owner, you are also responsible for finding the right manufacturer that can provide you with your orders in bulk. Again, research is your most powerful tool. It is also necessary that you have enough funds to make a bulk order from the manufacturer, pay Amazon fees, and cover miscellaneous expenses.

Setting up an Amazon account and registering for their Amazon FBA service is also your sole responsibility. Creating your own brand (e.g. coming up with your brand name and logo), prepping the products, adding your listings, monitoring your inventory, tracking your shipment, filing your tax, and so on are just some additional responsibilities of the seller. You can also choose your own freight forwarder to have the products shipped out to Amazon.

2. The manufacturer

Once you have found the manufacturer that meets all your business requirements, you can now contact them and start doing business with them under a contract that both of you agreed upon. Your chosen supplier is responsible for manufacturing the items that you ordered—whether it is 1,000 units of funny hats or 500 pieces of planners. If you have your own design that you want to sell, you can contact a manufacturer who can make the products for you according to your own specifications. If you just have an idea but you have not created a design of your own, you can simply find a manufacturer through different channels such as Alibaba, which is basically like China's Amazon.

You pay for the finished products, which means that the manufacturer is responsible for finding the materials required for making the products and paying for the workers who are going to make the products. All of these are accounted for when they quote you a price. Once the products are finished, the manufacturer has to find a shipping company to have your orders delivered either to you or directly to Amazon. It's all up to you.

3. Amazon

The third key player in this whole business model is, of course, Amazon. Whether you decide to sell via FBA or FBM (stands for fulfilled by merchant, meaning you just use Amazon as an online selling platform but you take care of the fulfillment aspect), you still need to use Amazon's services. Amazon's involvement begins when you decide to sell your products through their website. After registering, you need to send your items to their fulfillment centers. You can choose to ship using Amazon's partner shippers. With the FBA business model, Amazon has added responsibilities, such as storage of your goods, sorting, shipping to customers, and handling customer complaints and returns.

4. Shippers

The shippers are responsible for moving the products from the manufacturer to you as the seller or to Amazon's fulfillment center. They are also responsible for shipping the orders to the customer, and reverse shipping in case the customer wants to return or exchange the product. Basically, shipping the products to one of Amazon's fulfillment centers can be done by the manufacturer or by the seller. It can be a little tricky if your manufacturer is located overseas, like in China, because shipping can be more expensive, especially if you decide to do air freight.

The better option for international shipping is sea freight, especially if the items are big and heavy. It is cheaper but it takes much longer for the items to reach their destination. If you have the products with you, you also have the option to use traditional courier services such as FedEx or UPS via Amazon Partnered Carrier Program.

And when a customer buys the product, Amazon will deliver the order using their partner courier, mainly UPS, or FedEx and DHL in places that are not serviced by UPS.

5. Inspectors and prep services

Prepping your products to be shipped to Amazon can be challenging because Amazon has strict requirements. To make your life easier, you can simply hire inspectors and prep companies to do these things for you. These companies are responsible for inspecting the items to ensure that they are not damaged or counterfeit and that they adhere to Amazon's strict standards, packing of products, labeling, sorting, photography of products, and forwarding of shipment to Amazon fulfillment centers. This is especially useful if you are buying from a manufacturer which is located overseas or far from where you live. The prepping company and inspector will ensure that the goods are in good condition and they are packaged, labeled, and sorted according to Amazon's requirements. This saves you a lot of time and trouble because goods that do not pass the standards of Amazon's warehouses will be sent back to the manufacturer or the seller, depending on where it came from. Some examples of these companies are FBAinspection, FBAshipuk, and McKenzie services, to name a few. These companies ensure that your products are perfect before they are shipped to Amazon.

You have the option not to hire the services of inspectors and prep companies but if you want to make sure that the whole process will go smoothly, it is best to work with these professionals. This is especially helpful for sellers who have to prepare a high volume of orders. As a seller, it is your responsibility to communicate with the manufacturer and prepping companies the schedule and timings of pickup or delivery.

6. Others

Aside from these, you might also want to hire someone who will create your brand logo. This is an important step that a lot of private label sellers take for granted, thinking they can just use any logo that they come up with. Your brand is important, and it is best to hire a professional graphic designer who can make your brand logo. If you have the talent to do these kinds of things, then go ahead and make your own logo. If not, and all you can do is create random shapes in Paint, then the best thing for you to do is hire a professional. You can hire plenty of good professionals from Fiverr or Upwork. Searching the keyword "*Logo Design*" on Fiverr will bring up a list of freelancers, go through their portfolio and reviews and choose one that meets your taste and budget.

Once your company grows, you should also consider hiring a professional number cruncher a.k.a. an accountant. He will be responsible for balancing your business' books to check how much you are earning, and if you are earning in the first place. This is a must, especially if you are shelling out thousands of dollars to start this business. You also do not want to get in trouble by filing the wrong tax forms and returns. All of these can be done by your accountant.

Pretty soon, as your company continues to grow, you should also think about hiring your own lawyer, who can look over your contracts with manufacturers and suppliers, and also who can give you legal advice in case somebody decided to sue you for something. You might also need to hire your own staff or assistance who can do menial tasks for you so that you can focus on more important things. All of these are a must once your business becomes huge and you start earning hundreds of thousands of dollars.

Books In The Business and Money Series	
Series #	**Book Title**
1	Affiliate Marketing
2	Passive Income Ideas
3	Affiliate Marketing + Passive Income Ideas (2-in-1 Bundle)
4	Facebook Advertising
5	Dropshipping
6	Dropshipping + Facebook Advertising (2-in-1 Bundle)
7	Real Estate Investing For Beginners
8	Credit Cards and Credit Repair Secrets
9	Real Estate Investing And Credit Repair Strategies (2-in-1 Bundle)
10	Passive Income With Affiliate Marketing (2nd Edition)
11	Passive Income With Dividend Investing
12	Stock Market Investing For Beginners
13	The Simple Stock Market Investing Blueprint (2-in-1 Bundle)
14	Real Estate And Stock Market Investing Mastery (3-in-1 Bundle)

The kindle edition will be available to you for FREE when you purchase the

paperback version from Amazon.com (The US Store)

Download The Audio Versions Along With The Complementary PDF Document For FREE from

www.MichaelEzeanaka.com > My Audiobooks

Chapter 2

Getting Started

Now that you have an idea about how Amazon FBA works, you should now learn the step-by-step procedure for getting started on your e-commerce business. It is not as difficult as you think. Maybe as you are starting, you find it a bit challenging with all the people, tools, and processes involved. But as you progress, the entire process will become second nature to you. And the more you feel comfortable doing it, the more efficient your business will be.

Steps on how to start private label selling via Amazon FBA

This is assuming that you already have the money to start a business, because it's easier to progress when you have the financial wherewithal. If you haven't got the money, don't worry. The last chapter of the book, **Credit Card And Credit Repair Secrets** goes into detail with regards to different sources of funds you can explore for your business.

Later on, you will get a lot of information regarding the costs and fees involved in starting an Amazon FBA private label business. For now, here are the things that you need to do to get started. Although each of these will be discussed in length and depth in the next few chapters, you still need to have a clear idea of the step-by-step procedure that you need to do to start a private label business via Amazon FBA.

1. Determine the product that you want to sell

This requires a lot of brainstorming and research on your end. You cannot just simply start selling a product because that's what you like - although selling something that you like is also important because it adds passion to what you do. You should be selling products that the market demands for. Otherwise, no one will buy your goods.

You can research about the types of products that are selling online. Your first stop should be Amazon itself. Check the different categories and look for interesting products. There is one category called "Hot New Releases" and you might just be able to get ideas from here. You can also simply Google the top-selling products on Amazon. You can also look for unique products in different social media platforms. Check the pages of popular influencers and find out what they are currently using or wearing.

Sometimes, inspiration will strike when you are not looking for it, maybe when you are window-shopping in your favorite boutique or even when you are having a conversation with your friend. You will know and feel when your idea is worth pursuing because you will feel excited to start your business.

2. Look for a manufacturer or supplier

Now that you already have an idea about the kind of product that you want to sell, you should now start searching for a supplier who can manufacture the products for you. If you can find a manufacturer or a supplier in your area, lucky you because you can easily visit the company in person and check the products that they make. You can also talk to them in person, which makes it easier to communicate your needs. If not, you can always check overseas suppliers.

A lot of Amazon private label sellers get their products from manufacturers located in China. How do they find these Chinese suppliers? Through Alibaba, AliExpress etc. Alibaba is like the yellow pages of Chinese manufacturers. You can contact the manufacturer through the app. You will see the retail price per unit and the minimum number of orders that they accept. You can also ask for a sample if you want to see if the quality of their products is up to your standards. It is best to contact more than one supplier, maybe 3 to 5, just to give you more options and to get the best deal.

3. Finalize your brand

While you are waiting for your products, you can use your time creating your brand. That is, if you have not created it before you started searching for the product. You might already have a vague idea of what you want your brand to look like but you still need to finalize everything. Since you are selling private label products, you can put your brand name or logo on the packaging or on the product itself. In some cases, it is best to already have a finalized brand name and logo so that the manufacturer can already add it to your product, for example, if you are planning to sell clothes. If not, you can always use other ways to incorporate your brand to the product.

You can maybe add a sticker or a tag that carries your brand name and logo. You can also design your own packaging, although it will still be hidden inside the poly bags that Amazon requires you to use and the final layer of packaging for when the item is going to be shipped to the customer. You should try to include your shop's contact details on the packaging or tag, such as website URL, phone numbers, social media pages, and other useful information that will lead the customer to your shop.

4. Create your Amazon account

This may be complicated for some people, but you have to master the Amazon website because this will be your selling platform. All you need to do is to go to the website and sign up if you do not have an Amazon seller account yet. If you do, you still need to create your Amazon FBA account by simply going to the Amazon FBA home page. The step-by-step procedure for creating your Amazon FBA account will be discussed later on in this chapter.

5. List your items

After creating your Amazon seller account, you can now start adding your listings. You can do this even when the products haven't arrived yet as long as you already have the photos and the specifications of the products. Be sure to tick the box that says you want Amazon to ship your products and to provide customer service to take advantage of Amazon FBA.

6. Prepare your inventory

Once the manufacturer is done with your orders, you can now start preparing your inventory to be shipped to Amazon's fulfillment center. You can hire a prepping company to do this for you, as discussed previously. Or you can do it yourself if you think you can follow Amazon's policies regarding product prepping.

7. Ship your items

Your products are now ready to be shipped to Amazon. Once your products arrive at Amazon's fulfillment centers, your listing will become active.

Once your products reach Amazon's warehouse, the rest of the process is pretty much Amazon's responsibility. You can sit back and wait for the orders to come in, but it is also important to keep promoting and advertising your business so that your products and brand will become more visible.

How to create an Amazon seller central account

This is what will connect you to Amazon. You cannot do business with them without an account, especially if you are planning to sell via FBA. Assuming that you don't have an account with Amazon yet, here are the steps that you need to follow.

1. Go to Amazon website

Just go to this website URL and click the Start selling button. Since you do not have an account yet, just click the Create your Amazon account button and enter the following details: your name, your email address (it is better to use a business email address, which is different from your personal email), and password (should be at least 6 characters).

2. Professional vs. individual

You need to choose what type of account you want to have as a seller—professional or individual. You might say, of course the obvious choice is professional because this is your business. However, it is important to note the differences between the two so that you can choose which plan will work best for you.

For both plants, you will have the option to sell via FBA. The main difference between the two is the number of items that you can sell per month. If you are going to sell more than 40 items per month, then it is best to choose the professional account. If your inventory will only have less than 40 items per month, then choose individual account. A professional seller plan also has a monthly fee of $39.99 per month while an individual seller plan doesn't require you to pay an upfront fee. However, individual sellers are required to pay $0.99 every time they sell an item. This fee is waived for professional sellers. If you are confident that your items will sell like hotcakes, then go ahead and pay for the professional seller plan.

If you are not yet sure, you can always try the individual seller plan first, then later on upgrade to professional plan as you start getting the hang of selling on Amazon.

3. Seller information

The details that you need to provide after creating a username and password are your legal name (for taxation purposes), the name of your business (or your display name) and the website URL (if you are already selling online), and your contact number (mobile or telephone). You can choose whether you want to receive a phone call or an SMS for your PIN verification. Read the seller agreement and tick the box. If you are an international seller, meaning you don't reside in the US, you need to read additional important information, which is also on the same page.

When asked to provide your business display name, it is best to use your brand name because this is the one that buyers will see next to your items. It should represent the kind of products that you sell and it should also be easy to remember.

Click next.

4. Verification

You will receive a phone call or a text message to verify your phone number and your account.

5. Set up your billing method

You also need to provide your credit card details for billing and bank account details for deposits. Just give your bank account number and routing number that you can find in the package given to you when you first opened your bank account or if you already lost it, you can just contact your bank. You will also see here your selling plan (professional vs. individual) and the corresponding fees that you need to pay. This is also the part where you can choose Amazon FBA as a way of selling.

6. Provide your tax information

This is a mandatory step and basically, it is just like filling out your W-9 form. You will be asked different questions about your tax information such as the income beneficiary, if you are a U.S.

citizen, your name as shown on your income tax return, and your federal tax classification. This will be validated by Amazon.

7. Product information

This is an optional step for account setup. You can do this later if you are pressed for time. The questions that you will be asked are if you have Universal Product Codes (UPC) for your items, if you manufacture and brand your products, and the number of different products that you want to sell. Voila! Your Amazon seller account is now set up! The next step is exploring your seller central space, which is all about managing your inventory and orders. This is where you will add your listings. It has several tabs that include Inventory, Pricing, Orders, Advertising, Reports, and Performance.

What tools are required?

When it comes to selling online, you will have a lot of options with regards to different tools that you can use to help you boost your brand and sales. These tools also help you run your business more smoothly and efficiently. Some of the tools that you should know as an Amazon FBA seller are as follows:

For niche research

If you have a product in mind and you want to know if it has a good market, you can use certain software for niche research such as Viral Launch. It'll help you find the best ideas with regards to what products to sell, sales estimates for these products, competitor tracking, opportunity scores (products that are considered good opportunities will be given a high score), and many more. You cannot simply rely on your gut instinct when it comes to choosing the best products to sell, especially if a lot of money is involved.

For keyword research

In the world of online selling, keyword is KING. You may have the best products, but if you are not using the right keywords for them, people will still not see them. You need to familiarize yourself with

SEO and how it works in online selling. <u>Viral Launch</u> also provides keyword research assistance. You can also try <u>Merchant Words</u>, <u>Keyword Tool</u> and <u>Sonar-tool</u>.

For URL shortener

You do not want to scare your customers away by giving them links that are too long, and include so many weird looking characters. You should shorten your URLs using software such as Bitly and Google Short URL.

For calculating profit margins, fees, etc.

There is a tool called FBA Calculator for Amazon (you can't get any more specific than that!) that helps you calculate your profit margins. Calculating your profit margins while selling via Amazon FBA is not as simple as calculating typical profit margins because there is a lot of fees involved. There is also a specific calculator for freight rate called Amazon FBA Freight Rate Calculator.

For managing feedbacks and reviews

This type of software helps boost your rating as a seller because it helps you send feedback request emails to customers. Sometimes, customers do not make an effort to write a review when they purchase a product because no one is urging them to do it. When they receive an email from you asking them to write a review, they will remember and will be more than willing to do it because you made a specific request. One example of this type of software is AMZFinder. It gives you 500 free auto-emails per month that will help you receive more positive reviews, which can in turn boost your sales and improve your ranking.

For managing reimbursements

Amazon may be a huge company that has topnotch facilities and efficient staff but just like all companies, they still make mistakes. Sometimes, these mistakes can cost sellers money. Maybe they mishandled a product and when the customer received it, it's already damaged. Or maybe they unknowingly received a counterfeit item from another seller, and they sent out this particular item to your buyer, and when the buyer received the item, he understandably returned the item and asked for a refund. Things like these can happen, and it is a normal part of running a business. But you can minimize your losses using software such as AMZ Refund and Refunds Manager that help manage eligible reimbursements.

For multi-channel selling and inventory management

If you are selling on other platforms and websites, or if you have a high volume of inventory, you should consider using a tool that will help you manage all your listings. They will let you know when you are running low on supplies so that you can restock. They can also help integrate multiple online selling platforms into one system to make it easier for you to track your sales, orders, and inventory. Some examples of these software are Brightpearl, RestockPro, and Forecastly.

For product content optimization

Sometimes, duplicate content makes it difficult for search engines to choose which version is more relevant. Search engines also penalize duplicate contents, which is why some pages do not get high rankings even though they have similar content to those that are on the first few pages. Maybe you have been penalized by Google, and you just don't know it. Certain tools can help you with these kinds of issues such as Content26, Geek Speak Commerce, and mobiReady.

For pricing solutions

In such a huge market platform like Amazon, you will surely have several competitors, no matter how unique your niche may be. And if there are multiple sellers selling the same product, where will the buyer take his business? To the seller which offers the lowest price. This is also what you will do if you are the buyer. This is why it is important to monitor and compare prices of the kinds of products that you sell. You can use certain tools designed for this such as Price Checker 2.0, Appeagle, and Feedvisor.

For product launch

You need to launch your product, especially since you are a private label seller. The main goal of doing a product launch is to let people know about your products and also about your brand. Certain tools can help you with this such as Viral Launch, SnagShout, and iLoveToReview.

For accessing online courses, mentors, and community of sellers

Beginners like you will benefit a lot if you have someone who can give you advice regarding selling on Amazon. If you have extra money, you can hire a mentor in consulting marketplaces such as Clarity, where you have to pay per amount of time spent with the mentor. For an online course, you can try Proven Amazon Course, which includes Proven Private Label. You can also search for online communities of Amazon sellers. Some forums that you should check out are Ecommerce Fuel, Amazon Seller Central, and Reddit's Fulfillment by Amazon Subreddit.

These are the basic tools that can help you with your journey as a beginning Amazon private label seller. You will find out what tools you *really* need as you start selling.

What are the costs involved in selling via Amazon FBA?

1. Sourcing the product

This is the initial cost that you need to cover because without products, you will not be able to start your business. The product cost depends on the number of units you want to order from the manufacturer. Since you are a beginner and you do not want to shell out tens of thousands of dollars right away, let's assume that you only want to order about 200 to 300 units of the product that you have in mind.

Wholesale orders usually run from $0.50 to $10 each unit. This is again dependent on the kind of product that you want to order. Let's say you want to order 300 units of canvas bags with fun prints and the price of each unit is $2 each. You have to pay $600 to the manufacturer. The cost of sourcing your product is less than $1000.

2. Shipping

You still need to do a little shipping even if you are selling via Amazon FBA. You need to ship the items to Amazon and you can use your own courier if you want to. Shipping fees depend on how you want the items to be shipped—by air or sea. Air cargo is more expensive than sea cargo, although air is much faster than sea. This is why people who want to expedite the delivery of something usually use air cargo. If your products have regular size and weight, the typical computation of the shipping fee is about 60% to 80% of the cost of the product. This percentage already includes the courier fees and the declared value of your items. Going back to the example in the previous point, if your manufactured products cost $600, your shipping cost would be around $360 to $480.

3. Branding and logo

This is an optional cost, but if you want your brand and logo to look professional, you might want to hire someone who can do it for you, unless of course you are good at doing such kinds of things. You can easily hire someone to work on your branding and logo on Fiverr. You just need to pay $5 (hence the name Fiverr). Aside from Fiverr, you can also search for freelancers on other sites (e.g. upwork). They can provide you with your logo and packaging design. Let's say you will spend around $50 for this.

4. Photography

Online selling requires great photos of your products because this is what your future customers will see. Although this is also an optional cost, having professionally done photos will make your products stand out among the rest. You will notice the difference when you browse through the different listings. It might be easier these days to take great photos even by just using your phone's camera but it is still a better idea to have professional-looking pictures.

These professionals know things than an amateur photographer might not know such as the right way to take pictures of certain items, lighting, and so on. Again, you can use the same website that you used for finding a freelance graphic designer. You might have 300 items but they are more or less the same so you do not really need to take a picture of each. Let's just say for all the photos that you need, maybe 10 different shots, you have to pay $100.

5. Online tools and software

These include product and keyword research tools, calculators, profit monitoring software, product tracking software, pricing tools, and so on. For beginners, you probably won't get all of these software tools at once. You will probably only get the one with the most features, say, Viral Launch. They offer different packages for beginners which cost $29, intermediate for $59, and pro for $99. If you decide to get the intermediate version like most sellers, you have to pay $59.

6. Inspection service

This is another optional cost because this depends on how much you trust your supplier. If your products are simple, like canvas bags, then hiring a company that provides inspection services is not necessary. But if your product is kind of complicated and the manufacturer is from abroad, you might want to have your products professionally inspected. This will cost you around $100 to $300.

7. UPC barcode

You can send a UPC barcode to the supplier so that you can have it printed on your products before they get sent out to Amazon. This will cost around $5.

8. Running ads

As a seller, you have the option to have your products sponsored. You can choose products and keywords that you want to appear for on Amazon's specific pages such as product detail pages and in search results. The cost of sponsored products and brands depends on how many times your ads get clicked. You can also set the budget that you want to spend for your ads. To give you an idea, the minimum daily budget for keyword targeted ads is $1.

9. Amazon costs

Amazon will not be doing all of these for free. There must be some fees involved. And you are right. In fact, Amazon sellers pay a lot of different fees for different purposes.

Product fees

There are three types of product fees that sellers pay to Amazon.

- Referral fee - 6% to 20%, average is 15%, based on category and selling price

- Minimum referral fee - $0-$2, if referral fee is smaller than minimum fee, based on category

- Variable closing fee- $1.80, for all media categories

To illustrate, let's say for instance you are selling 4 pieces of mugs for $5.99. The 15% referral fee would be $0.89 and the minimum fee for this category is $1. Since the referral fee of $0.89 is smaller than the minimum fee of $1, you will pay $1 to Amazon. Let's take another example. If you are selling a set of four fleece blankets for $24.99, your referral fee will be $3.75, which is bigger than the minimum fee of $1. In this example, you will pay the $3.75 referral fee.

Variable closing fee is a flat rate of $1.80 no matter how much the product costs. This will be added on top of the referral fee. Some examples of media categories where you have to pay variable closing fees are video games, video game consoles, software, music, DVD, and books.

Seller account fees

As discussed earlier, there are two types of seller accounts—individual and professional. Individual seller accounts have no monthly fees, but they have to pay a $0.99 listing fee when the item is sold. This account is ideal for occasional sellers. On the other hand, professional sellers, or those volume sellers and businesses, have to pay $39.99 per month, but they no longer need to pay $0.99 per listing.

Amazon FBA fees

The two major fees that you will pay if you decide to use FBA are:

- Fees for picking, packing, and shipping

- Monthly fees for storage (which means that the longer your products stay in the fulfillment centers, the higher your fees will be)

These fees are based on the size and weight of your products. They divide the product size into two categories—standard size and oversize. Any item with dimension less than 18"x14"x8" and weighs less than 20 pounds once packaged are considered standard-sized. Oversize products, on the other hand, are anything exceeding the dimension and weight mentioned above.

Amazon further divides each of these product size categories:

Standard-size:

- Small standard size that weighs 1 lb or less- $2.41
- Large standard size that weighs 1 lb or less- $3.19
- Large standard size that weighs 1 to 2 lbs- $4.71
- Large standard size that weighs over 2 lbs- $4.71 for first 2 lbs + $0.38 per additional lb

Oversize:

- Small oversize- $8.13 for first 2 lbs + $0.38 per additional lb
- Medium oversize- $9.44 for first 2 lbs + $0.38 per additional lb
- Large oversize- $73.18 for first 90 lbs + $0.79 per additional lb
- Special oversize- $137.32 for first 90 lbs + $0.91 per additional lb

The abovementioned fees include picking, packing, handling, shipping, customer service, and returns. Storage fees, on the other hand, are based on the volume of your inventory and the calendar months.

Standard size:

- Jan-Sept: $0.64 per cubic foot
- Oct-Dec: $2.35 per cubic foot

Oversize:

- Jan-Sept- $0.43 per cubic foot
- Oct-Dec- $1.15 per cubic foot

These are the basic fees that you need to know as an Amazon FBA seller.

Books In The Business and Money Series	
Series #	**Book Title**
1	Affiliate Marketing
2	Passive Income Ideas
3	Affiliate Marketing + Passive Income Ideas (2-in-1 Bundle)
4	Facebook Advertising
5	Dropshipping
6	Dropshipping + Facebook Advertising (2-in-1 Bundle)
7	Real Estate Investing For Beginners
8	Credit Cards and Credit Repair Secrets
9	Real Estate Investing And Credit Repair Strategies (2-in-1 Bundle)
10	Passive Income With Affiliate Marketing (2nd Edition)
11	Passive Income With Dividend Investing
12	Stock Market Investing For Beginners
13	The Simple Stock Market Investing Blueprint (2-in-1 Bundle)
14	Real Estate And Stock Market Investing Mastery (3-in-1 Bundle)
	The kindle edition will be available to you for FREE when you purchase the paperback version from Amazon.com (The US Store)

Download The Audio Versions Along With The Complementary PDF Document For FREE from

www.MichaelEzeanaka.com > My Audiobooks

Chapter 3

Product Research

Given that your product is the heart and soul of your business, it's very important you research what kind of products will sell well on Amazon. Here are some tips that you need to know when it comes to choosing the right product for your business.

Criteria for selecting a good product

1. Good demand

You have probably learned this in basic economics. For your business to flourish, there should be a good demand for the products you are selling. You have to understand that demand sells. One of the reasons why a product is not selling is because there is no demand for it, meaning people do not want or need it. Another is that you have overestimated its demand, which led you to overprice the product. Or maybe you are simply selling your products to the wrong market. Having a high demand for your products will surely lead to high sales. If you already bought your products and you realized later on that the demand for them is quite low, you can still do something about it by artificially creating a demand.

One way to create an artificial demand is through *exclusivity*. Ever wonder why Apple products are highly sought-after even if they are extremely expensive? One reason is exclusivity. For one, they are expensive, which means only people with that kind of money can afford them. Second, Apple does not release products left and right, unlike its competitors. Third, they have their own tech centers, app stores, and so on. This makes the owners of Apple products feel exclusive.

You cannot simply increase the price of your products, or sell them to certain groups of people. You can instead use other techniques, such as selling "limited edition" items. Or, you can sell certain items at a limited time only. This makes potential buyers think that your products are scarce, that if they don't buy one now, they might not have the chance to buy later. You can also offer incentives to first time buyers to increase demand.

2. Not too much competition

Finding a good product that has a high demand but does not have a lot of competitors is a dilemma that most sellers face. After all, if a product is in demand, a lot of business owners will surely want to sell them. Certain types of products such as clothing and shoes are already highly saturated by a lot of sellers.

You need to find a product that has a demand but does not have a lot of sellers that offer them. One such product is a niche product. There is probably a large group of people out there looking for certain types of products that typical businesses don't sell. For example, clothing is an in demand product, but there is too much competition. But, if you really want to sell clothes, you should find ways to tweak your product a bit to make it unique and original that will sell to a certain group of people. For example, you can sell vintage-style swimsuits instead of the regular swimsuits. You can also sell kinky outfits for couples who love to do role play sex.

These are under the clothing category, but you are targeting a niche. Another popular niche clothing product is vegan or sustainable clothes. You will still have competition, but it won't be too high as compared to mainstream types of clothes like what H & M or Forever21 sells.

3. Not too seasonal

Seasonal products are those that are in demand during a particular season such as Easter, Christmas, Fourth of July, Halloween, etc. Seasonal products are highly profitable if you are selling them at the right time. When they are no longer in season, these products will sit in the Amazon shelves for months, collecting dust and accumulating storage fees. This is why you should avoid buying a lot of seasonal products for reselling, such as decors, costumes, or treats. Do not spend thousands of dollars on these items because they will surely sit for a long time in storage. You can still buy seasonal products but only a limited amount and you should also know when you should start buying them – timing is critical.

If you really want to sell seasonal products, maybe you can sell something that will cover different seasons. For example, fairy lights can be a great Christmas décor, but they are also used by a lot of people as regular room décor. You can also sell generic gift baskets that can be given as gifts on Mother's Day, Christmas, graduation, and so on.

4. Affordable retail price

You might think selling high-priced items is the best way to go if you want to earn a high profit, but you are wrong because it is still best to choose products that you can sell at an affordable retail price. For example, if you decide to sell private labeled watches that have Swarovski crystals on them, this will cost you a lot of capital, which means that you have to sell them at an even higher price if you want to earn a profit.

People may not be willing to spend hundreds of dollars on a brand that they have not heard of. This is why you should sell affordable products as you are establishing your brand. Moreover, expensive items can sit for a long time in storage because people are generally more cautious when it comes to buying more expensive items. If you sell them products that will only cost them a few dollars, they will not even think twice, and just simply click the buy now button even if they don't really need it and without researching about it.

5. Fewer reviews

You might think that selling a product with a lot of reviews is a great idea because it means that a lot of people are buying them. Although this can be true, it also means that the market is highly saturated because there is already a lot of sellers selling the same product. A product with fewer reviews means that it does not have a lot of sellers yet. It is still an untapped market that has a lot of potential.

6. Room for improvement

Selling a perfect product may not be a great idea because it means that nothing else can be done with it. It is already the final and ultimate version of that product. No more improvement can be made, which means that the price remains the same. Although there is no such thing as a perfect product (after all, nothing is perfect in this world), there are still products that give you very little room for improvement.

The design or structure of the product is not something that you can tweak to modify. This is not a good kind of product to sell, especially for private label sellers because you cannot add any value to it to make it your own. You should choose a product that gives you a lot of wiggle room, a product that gives you enough space for creativity. In one of the examples given before, selling canvas bags is a good idea because it allows you to customize different designs and prints.

7. Not in gated categories

There are certain types of products that require sellers to get Amazon's permission before they can start selling them on the website. There is an approval process that sellers need to go through if they want to sell products under the gated category, which is why this is not a good product to sell on Amazon, especially for startups. Amazon has to "gate" certain items to protect their reputation, especially since the number of third-party sellers have increased dramatically over the last few years. This is Amazon's way of protecting their reputation. They do not want to have counterfeit or low quality products being sold on their website. Some examples of gated categories are fine jewelry, DVDs, watches, grocery items and gourmet food, fine arts, collectibles, and automotive. During the holiday season, Amazon also gates toys and games.

8. Not likely to attract litigations

You should also choose products that are not likely to get you sued. First, you need to know the kinds of products that attract litigations. Some examples are food, vitamins, cosmetics, and anything that you put inside your body or apply on your skin or hair. If you want to avoid litigations, you better choose products that are not applied on the body, eaten, taken orally, or inserted inside the body. Choose something easy and safe, such as canvas bags, pens, clothes, notebooks, blankets, and so on. There are thousands of products to choose from that are not likely to attract litigations. These types of products are for sellers or brands that are already established, such as Kylie Cosmetics or Hershey's. These are large corporations that have a team of lawyers handling these litigations. You, on the other hand, are a one-man team who is just starting and cannot afford (yet) to hire your own business lawyer.

9. Not too fragile

If you are a very patient person and money is not an issue, go ahead and sell products that easily break such as eyeglasses, ceramic mugs, plates, light bulbs, and so on. Selling these products can lead to a lot of returns because they get damaged easily, either during transit or while in storage. No matter how the product gets broken, you still have to process the return and refund or exchange and this is a lot to handle, especially if you are processing multiple return transactions. Just imagine if all of your products are easily breakable. You will probably spend more time and money processing returns than selling the product itself.

Five best selling categories on Amazon

Since you are planning to sell on Amazon, you should also know the best-selling categories on the website. This will give you an idea about the kinds of products that you can sell that will give you the highest sales volume and profits.

1. Books

It all started when Jeff Bezos, the founder of Amazon, started selling books online. This is why books are one of the top selling categories on Amazon. Books are Amazon's very first product category. We are not talking about digital books here. We are talking about the traditional kind made of paper and ink. You might think, are there still people reading physical books? Aren't there e-books that they can easily download on their Kindle and iPad? Yes, there are still a lot of readers who prefer paper books over e-books. This is why this is still a huge market. Moreover, books have a large profit margin.

You can buy books wholesale for just one dollar, give or take a few cents. And you know how much one paper book costs. You can mark up your book items at 1000% of the original price. Selling books on Amazon may not be something that you can consider as your major source of income, but it is definitely one of the most stable categories on Amazon that has a huge market, and will definitely give you a solid income regularly.

2. Workout clothes

These days, a lot of people enjoy doing physical activities — going to the gym, running, yoga, and so on. This makes exercise clothing one of the highest selling categories on Amazon. People want to be comfortable and at the same time look good while doing their favorite workout, especially since they take a picture of themselves wearing their exercise gear and post it on social media. In fact, the popularity of exercising and working out gave birth to a fashion trend called athleisure.

You will now see a lot of people wearing workout clothes not only in the gym or while exercising, but also when going to the grocery or even to parties. You see them wearing sports bra with leggings and running shoes everywhere. And despite the increasing number of people who buy second hand clothes, a lot of them still prefer brand new workout clothes. Nobody wants to wear a pair of used leggings or sports bra. It is a huge market right now, and you should definitely take advantage of that. The only downside is that it is hard to find a manufacturer that can make high quality athleisure clothes. Low quality workout clothes are not comfortable to wear, and comfort is one of the things that you should look out for when it comes to buying workout clothes. You should also be aware of the characteristics of the workout clothes that you should be selling. There are clothes that absorb sweat or pull sweat away from the body. You also have to pick workout clothes for different physical activities and seasons.

3. Electronic items and accessories

For Amazon FBA sellers, electronic items might be difficult to sell because people would generally buy electronics from a well-established and known brand. What you can do instead is to just find electronic accessories to sell. You can sell a wide variety of accessories for different electronics— phone cases, laptop sleeves, laptop bags, phone pouches, power banks, memory cards, screen protectors, and so on. You can easily find a manufacturer for these. All you need to do is to find one that offers the best deal. There are a lot of different electronic devices that come out every few months and you can be sure that people will buy accessories for these.

However, having new devices come out every month is a double-edged sword. It is a positive thing for sellers because it means more things and varieties to sell for them. It is also a negative thing because devices get replaced fast, which means that you might still have some accessories for a device that is already obsolete. The key here is to monitor trends and do not buy too many items for one particular device.

4. Baby items

Baby items are always in demand because humans always procreate. And babies need a lot of stuff. In fact, they need more stuff than adults. Their stuff also get replaced fast because babies grow and develop fast, unlike an adult who can own and wear the same clothes for ten years. One advantage of selling baby items is that they are usually small and lightweight, unless of course you are selling baby furniture. They are also inexpensive, which can give you a huge profit margin. However, you should avoid selling baby items that can get you sued such as baby food or feeding supplies. Just stick with regular items like clothing, toys, blankets, and so on.

5. Clothing, shoes, and jewelry

These are always in demand anywhere you go. People always buy clothes, shoes, and jewelry. Workout clothes have a separate category because it has its own huge market. However, there is still a lot of people who buy regular clothes, and also shoes and jewelry. Please note that this does not include jewelry made of precious metals such as solid gold and expensive materials such as Swarovski. These are regulated products and might be difficult to sell.

Clothing, shoes, and jewelry have always had a huge market whether it is online or in physical stores. You can also buy them in bulk for dirt-cheap because there are already a lot of manufacturers to choose from. They are also easy to ship because of their small size. You can never go wrong selling them. The only drawback is that because they are a popular category, you will have a lot of competition. This is why you need to add something to your products that will make them stand out from the rest. Maybe you can focus on selling only one type of clothes, such as sleepwear or lingerie. For shoes, maybe you can sell foldable flat shoes that they can easily store in their bags. For jewelry pieces, you can sell vintage-inspired jewelry that are quite popular these days.

These are the things that you need to consider when it comes to selling products on Amazon FBA. Once you find the product that you want to sell after careful research, you can now proceed to finding a reliable manufacturer or supplier who can make these products for you or sell them to you wholesale.

Books In The Business and Money Series	
Series #	**Book Title**
1	Affiliate Marketing
2	Passive Income Ideas
3	Affiliate Marketing + Passive Income Ideas (2-in-1 Bundle)
4	Facebook Advertising
5	Dropshipping
6	Dropshipping + Facebook Advertising (2-in-1 Bundle)
7	Real Estate Investing For Beginners
8	Credit Cards and Credit Repair Secrets
9	Real Estate Investing And Credit Repair Strategies (2-in-1 Bundle)
10	Passive Income With Affiliate Marketing (2nd Edition)
11	Passive Income With Dividend Investing
12	Stock Market Investing For Beginners
13	The Simple Stock Market Investing Blueprint (2-in-1 Bundle)
14	Real Estate And Stock Market Investing Mastery (3-in-1 Bundle)
The kindle edition will be available to you for FREE when you purchase the paperback version from Amazon.com (The US Store)	

Download The Audio Versions Along With The Complementary PDF Document For FREE from

www.MichaelEzeanaka.com > My Audiobooks

Chapter 4

Sourcing the Product

You should now search for the manufacturer or supplier where you can get your products from. This can be intimidating for a lot of people, especially beginners because once you contact a supplier and order hundreds of units of an item, you can no longer back out or change your mind. You cannot simply say to the supplier that you do not want the items anymore after they started making them. You also cannot simply decide not to sell once you receive the products after spending hundreds or even thousands of dollars. What are you going to do with 100 pieces of baby clothes or 500 pieces of memo pads? Contacting a manufacturer signals the beginning of your business. You are already involving other groups of people, and you need to be professional about it.

Choosing a supplier may sound scary but it is not that difficult, especially today when everything is right at your fingertips. However, you should still be cautious because there are a lot of scammers out there, especially if you are ordering from abroad. To help you find and choose the right manufacturer or supplier for your business, here are some tips that you should know.

Where can you find suppliers?

These days, everything is made in China, and it is no wonder because there is a lot of manufacturers and suppliers of products in China. Although it is best to go to China and talk to the manufacturers in person, you can also simply contact them online. Here are some Chinese websites that you should check out.

https://www.alibaba.com/

This is probably the most popular website used by Amazon sellers. It is one of the biggest companies that do business with ecommerce sellers. Alibaba is based in China and has other websites—Tmall and Taobao. It is used by millions of people, including merchants, businesses, and individual sellers. Most of the people selling on Amazon get their products from Alibaba. Alibaba is like the yellow pages of manufacturers and suppliers. You will find here hundreds of companies that make products in bulk, usually by the hundreds. Their unit price is also dirt cheap, which gives you a chance to sell them at a higher mark up.

https://www.aliexpress.com/

Alibaba owns Aliexpress, and the two are not the same. The owner of Alibaba uses Aliexpress to compete against ecommerce giants such as Amazon and eBay. You can buy items per piece from Aliexpress, but not from Alibaba. However, you can still source your inventory from Alibaba because they offer their products at factory prices in smaller quantities.

https://www.made-in-china.com/

Founded in 1998, Made-In-China is also one of the leading B2B ecommerce websites in China. It works the same way as Alibaba, by bridging the gap between Chinese suppliers and international sellers. It makes it easier for people all over the world to contact Chinese manufacturers.

Aside from Chinese suppliers, you can also find manufacturers and suppliers in the US and Europe, although pricing can be a little more expensive.

Here are some websites that you should check out.

http://www.zentrada.eu/

This website is one of the largest sourcing platforms used by ecommerce sellers in Europe. Individual sellers are given new ideas for ordinary products that help them to succeed. Currently, they have around 400 thousand units of different products that come from different manufacturers, importers, and wholesalers worldwide.

http://www.koleimports.com/

If you live in Los Angeles, California, you can try contacting Kole Imports, a family-owned business in the US. It is one of the biggest general merchandisers and direct importers of different consumer goods. Established in 1985, Kole Imports gets their products directly from manufacturers abroad, and sell them in bulk to retailers and wholesalers. You can visit their website by clicking the link above or you can go to trade shows where they are participating.

http://www.closeoutfortune.dollardays.com/

Also based in the US, Closeoutfortune offers wholesale products at a low price. They have a wide assortment of products to choose from, and they also have a wide range of customers — non-profit groups, retailers, e-sellers, and even schools. They are a great source of items to sell, especially for small businesses and non-profit organizations.

How to evaluate reliability of suppliers

The knee-jerk reaction for most people searching for a supplier is to choose the one that offers the lowest price. This should not be the case because the most important thing is to find a supplier who can deliver what they promised. If you find a reliable supplier, you won't have to keep searching for new suppliers every time you need to replenish your inventory.

1. Main product

When choosing a manufacturer for your product, you need to make sure that the product you want them to make is their main product and not just something that they sell on the side. For example, if you are planning to sell bed sheets, you should go directly to a manufacturer that makes bed sheets, instead of going to a manufacturer that sells mainly mattresses but also makes bed sheets on the side.

2. Main markets for exports

Manufacturers whose main target markets are businesses in developed countries are generally more reliable than those whose target are businesses in developing countries. This is understandable because developed countries have stricter policies when it comes to product quality and safety standards. They closely monitor defects and compliance to regulations imposed by different government bodies.

3. Compliance to product safety

You also need to choose manufacturers that comply with product safety standards. As a seller, it is your responsibility to ensure that your products are safe to use by the general public. Some product safety regulations that you should know as a seller are electrical safety regulations, product packaging regulations, toys and children's products regulations, textile regulations, and so on. You need to know what regulations your intended product to sell should adhere to. And then, you need to find a manufacturer that makes products that will pass such regulations with flying colors.

Compliance to such standards is critical when it comes to importing from overseas, especially China because it can lead to product recalls, fines, seized cargos, and even litigations. This might even cause you millions of dollars, especially if the damage caused by your product is fatal and serious.

4. Quality management system

Monitoring the quality of the products that a manufacturer makes is a must in any manufacturing company. They have to closely monitor their products during and after production to minimize the number of units with defects. The higher the number of defective units, the lower the sales will be. This also has a negative impact on the manufacturer's reputation, which is why they try hard to keep their defects at a minimum. You need to find a supplier that follows QMS or quality management system. Unfortunately, only a small percentage, about 5% to 10% of manufacturers follows QMS. To find them, they should have an ISO certificate, usually ISO 9001.

5. Transparency

Manufacturers who are not willing to undergo factory audit or quality inspection probably have something to hide. You can eliminate unreliable manufacturers by telling them early on that you are going to do quality inspections and testing of samples. If they refuse, you should not do business with them because a reliable supplier will be more than willing to have these inspections.

Criteria to use when evaluating a supplier

Your business has its own specific needs, and you need to make sure that you choose a supplier that meets these needs. You need to create a list of criteria that will help you choose the one that will be able to provide you with the kind of products and service that you are looking for.

1. Cultural fit

The manufacturer should uphold the same cultural value that your business stands for. For instance, if you want to sell items made from bamboo because you want to promote the use of sustainable products and at the same time earn money through your business, you should find a manufacturer who adheres to the same principles.

2. Cost

The cost of everything—from the production of the goods to shipping—should be within your budget. You need to find a manufacturer that can offer you the lowest cost per unit but still maintains the quality of the products that you are looking for.

3. Order quantities

This depends on how many you want to order. Most manufacturers have a minimum order requirement. If you are just starting, you might want to choose a supplier that allows you to order by the hundreds, say, 300 units of the item.

4. Follows safety standards and quality control systems

The company should follow all the required regulations in terms of safety and quality standards imposed by the country where you live. You can ask for certifications, ISO numbers, and other permits to ensure that you are dealing with a legitimate supplier.

5. Turnaround time

How long can the manufacturer finish the product? The faster the products are finished, the faster you can launch your business. However, make sure that the short turnaround time will not negatively affect the quality of the products.

6. Flexibility

They should be willing to adjust if there are changes to be made to the orders and the product itself, of course with necessary pricing adjustments.

These are just some of the things that you should consider when choosing a manufacturer or supplier to do business with. These should be laid out before you decide to search for suppliers to ensure that you are choosing the right one for your business needs.

How To Spot Shady Suppliers

Hopefully, in your journey as an online seller, you will never come across a shady supplier or a scammer who only wants your money. These shady suppliers can be avoided by knowing the signs that you are dealing with one. Here are the things that you should look out for.

1. Too good to be true

You always hear the saying if it is too good to be true, it's probably not true. This also applies when choosing a manufacturer. If they promise to move heaven and earth just to finish your product within a very short period of time, and they are working on low capital because the quote that they gave you is too low, then this is probably not legit. Low price does not always mean a great deal. You might be dealing with a scammer who just wants to attract people to scam by giving them unbelievable deals.

2. Too much self-promotion but no substance

When you contact the supplier because you are attracted by their rates, and you notice that the supplier talks too much about all the great things that they can give you but you do not really see a lot of positive reviews from previous customers, chances are they are just building themselves up to make you sign that deal. A legit supplier will ask questions about the work that you want them to do and will show you proof of successes from previous clients.

3. Quote is too generic

When you ask for a quote, they should be able to give you the breakdown of everything and how they arrived at that amount for you to understand what you are paying for. A shady supplier will probably give you a cookie-cutter quote that he got from Google.

4. Hidden fees

If the pricing that they give you is vague, which gives them an opportunity to change the price in the future, you should be wary because you are probably dealing with a shady supplier. If they say something like "you need to pay us around 600 dollars, but we're not sure yet about the kind of materials you want and we can only find out once we start to make the products after you make the payment", you should back off because this is not how it should be done. A legitimate seller will give you an exact amount to be paid. After all, they are supposed to have been doing this for years, so they should know by now how much they should be charging their clients.

5. Delays in communication

Delays in responding to your calls or messages can mean that the supplier does not have a designated department for handling questions of potential clients or is simply too busy or disorganized. Either way, you wouldn't want to communicate with such a seller because it shows unreliability. This might cause problems in the future when you need to talk to them urgently and no one is responding.

Ordering samples

One way to ensure that you are getting products that meet your standards is to ask for samples from the manufacturer.

Why order samples?

To test the quality.

Pictures are sometimes not enough because they can be misleading. If you have the sample in your hand, you will be able to see, smell, and feel the actual product that you are going to buy and later on sell to your future customers.

To test the supplier.

This is also a great way to test the supplier. You will know if they are willing to send a sample and you will also find out how they communicate and work with their clients. You will also see their packaging and how fast they process and ship their orders.

To let them know that you are serious.

This is a subtle way to let them know that you are serious about your orders. Suppliers also weed out hundreds of "buyers" that don't actually order anything. This will let them know that you are willing to go further if you are satisfied with the sample.

How many samples should you order?

Ideally, you should order one sample per product that you will be ordering. However, you have to consider your budget and shipping fees because if you have a lot of different products, you might want to limit your order to a few samples. Maybe if you are ordering everything from one manufacturer, you can order a couple of samples just to see if their real products are the same as the ones in their picture. Some manufacturers will also not buy materials and spend time and money on labor just to make one item. You have to consider different aspects and make sure that you ask your supplier how you should go about ordering samples.

Why hire an inspector to check the products before shipment?

Although you might need to pay extra if you hire a professional inspector, you will at least get professional inspection of the products that you are going to sell. This is also cost effective in the long run because you don't have to go to the supplier's factory in person just to check your orders. This also means lower return rates because products meet the quality standards. Hiring an inspector is also beneficial because they would know what to look out for. After all, it is their job and they are trained to spot defects and subpar quality products that an ordinary person might miss. And inspectors like these are usually located in the same country as the manufacturer, which means easier communication among the supplier, the inspector, and you because the inspector can act as an intermediary.

Searching for the right supplier is not difficult as long as you know where to look and what to look for and look out for. The next chapter will teach you how to ship the products once the manufacturers are done with your orders.

Books In The Business and Money Series	
Series #	**Book Title**
1	Affiliate Marketing
2	Passive Income Ideas
3	Affiliate Marketing + Passive Income Ideas (2-in-1 Bundle)
4	Facebook Advertising
5	Dropshipping
6	Dropshipping + Facebook Advertising (2-in-1 Bundle)
7	Real Estate Investing For Beginners
8	Credit Cards and Credit Repair Secrets
9	Real Estate Investing And Credit Repair Strategies (2-in-1 Bundle)
10	Passive Income With Affiliate Marketing (2nd Edition)
11	Passive Income With Dividend Investing
12	Stock Market Investing For Beginners
13	The Simple Stock Market Investing Blueprint (2-in-1 Bundle)
14	Real Estate And Stock Market Investing Mastery (3-in-1 Bundle)
The kindle edition will be available to you for FREE when you purchase the paperback version from Amazon.com (The US Store)	

Download The Audio Versions Along With The Complementary PDF Document For FREE from

www.MichaelEzeanaka.com > My Audiobooks

Chapter 5

Shipping the Products

Once the manufacturer has completed your orders, the next step is to have them all shipped to Amazon FBA warehouses. You need to research this part before you place an order, especially if you decide to source your product from Chinese manufacturers because there is a lot of processes involved when it comes to importing items from abroad.

For illustration purposes, let's assume that your manufacturer is from China, where most Amazon FBA sellers get their inventory.

Shipping from China to Amazon Warehouse

There are three ways to ship form China to Amazon Warehouse:

- The items will be sent directly to Amazon Warehouse from China.
- The items will be sent to your home first and then to Amazon Warehouse.
- The items will be sent to a third-party company and then to Amazon Warehouse. This company will also check and prep the products for you.

Chinese supplier - Amazon Warehouse

A lot of people use this first method because it is the fastest and cheapest way among the three options for obvious reasons. This is especially true if you decide to use air or express cargo. You have to pay for the shipping fee twice if the products have to go through your home or a third-party company.

Chinese supplier - You - Amazon Warehouse

Some sellers prefer that they see the products that they ordered first hand before selling them online. This is especially helpful when it comes to ensuring that the items meet Amazon's quality requirements. This is also ideal if you live near the US main ports, like Los Angeles. It will add more to your shipping expenses if you live far from major ports because of the additional transportation costs from the port to your home. However, if you do decide to have the items shipped to your home first, you will be responsible for prepping your products, which can be a tedious process, especially for beginners like you.

Chinese supplier - Third-party – Amazon Warehouse

If you want your products to be inspected, prepped, and monitored professionally, and you have extra money to spare, you can hire a third-party company that can do all these things for you. You need to find a third-party company that is also located in the same state as the Amazon FBA warehouse if you want to have low shipping costs. If it is located in a different state, the shipping costs will be a lot more expensive.

Shipping by sea or air

1. Sea freight

This is a complicated method of shipping items for export and import because it involves a lot of steps. It may be complicated but it is still one of the major ways to transport products from one country to another because it can accommodate a large shipment at a much lower cost. The main disadvantage is the length of time. Shipping by sea has several stages:

- From the Chinese supplier to Chinese port (domestic)
- From the Chinese port to the US port (international, export and import)
- From the US port to your home, to the third-party company, or directly to Amazon FBA warehouse (domestic)

Two forwarders are involved in the entire process — the Chinese and US forwarders. They have to coordinate with each other and handle all the processes involving importing and exporting these goods to and from their respective countries.

You can either find your own freight forwarder or you can let your supplier find one for you. You need to understand that Amazon is not responsible for anything related to customs clearance and does not provide any delivery support. They also do not act as a contact for overseas customs clearance. These are all the responsibilities of the freight forwarder and also the seller. If your goods do not meet the requirements of the customs, they will be detained and the freight forwarder should know how to handle such scenarios.

Finding your own freight forwarder vs. letting your supplier find one for you

If you think you will continue having this business for many years to come, you might want to find a freight forwarder that you can rely on. Sounds cheesy, but that's how it should be. Moreover, finding your own forwarder is beneficial because you can find someone who speaks the same language as you do. And you are satisfied with what you have researched about them. You can choose someone who meets all your business needs. You can choose either a freight forwarder who is located in China or in the US, although the former is preferred by many. The main reason is the ease of communication, as stated previously, and there will also be no time difference that can affect communication because you live in the same state.

If you find your own freight forwarder, your Chinese supplier should deduct the cost from the total amount that you have to pay. The amount depends on whether the forwarder will ship from the supplier's warehouse or from a seaport in China.

Most beginners usually resort to the second option of letting their supplier find a freight forwarder for them because they do not have a lot of contacts yet. But as they continue doing their business, they will get recommendations from fellow sellers on where to find the best freight forwarder. But you can still choose to let your supplier handle the shipment process. This is especially a great idea if your supplier has done business with an Amazon seller before because they already know how it works. You do not have to explain about Amazon fulfillment centers, and the right way to prep the products. Just make sure to ask about the shipping costs because sometimes, they do not include the cost of shipping from the US port to Amazon.

The benefit of letting your supplier find a freight forwarder for you is that you do not need to search for it. And searching for freight forwarders and knowing what questions to ask can be challenging. With the expertise and connections of your supplier, you can be sure that you will have a reliable freight forwarder who can handle your shipment for you. The only downside is that you are not learning the nitty gritty of processing shipments and searching for your own contacts because you let your supplier do it for you.

Cost of sea freight

As mentioned earlier, there are a lot of steps involved when it comes to shipping goods by sea. However, it is still the cheapest way to ship because it can accommodate a large volume of shipment, unlike air freight, which has a limit. The cost of sea freight depends on *where the shipment is coming from, where it is going and what month you are going to ship.* But for reference, you can use $300/CBM which includes all shipping costs from a seaport in China to one of Amazon's warehouses located in the south of the USA. This will at least give you a rough estimate of how much you will be paying. The United States is a large country, and the shipping costs also depend on where you are located in the US. If the Amazon warehouse is in the west coast, the shipping fee will be much lower than if it is located in the east coast.

There is also a minimum shipping capacity when using sea freight, which is 2-3 CBM per shipment. Keep in mind that when using sea cargo, most of the fees and charges that the freight forwarders need to pay in the entire process of importing and exporting the goods are fixed no matter how much CBM shipment you have. The minimum is 2-3 CBM which is not difficult to reach since you are shipping goods in bulk.

Shipping time

So how long does it take for your cargo to reach Amazon's warehouse from China if you use sea freight? There are so many factors involved that it usually takes at least 30 days for a shipment to reach Amazon's warehouse located in the west coast coming from a Chinese seaport. If the Amazon warehouse is located in the east coast, it will take an additional 10 days, so 40 days in total. This is the minimum timeframe, but it could take longer than that. For example, if you ship during the holiday season in the US or during a festival in China, your cargo might take a longer time. There are also times when the customs clearance takes a longer time to complete because they are processing a higher volume of cargos than usual. Other factors that can affect the delivery time are the weather, labor issues at seaports, seasonal behaviors, and so on.

Christmas is the best time to sell online because a lot of people are buying gifts for their loved ones. So if you are planning to sell stuff for Christmas, you have to make sure that your shipment leaves China by the last week of October. If not, you will suffer delays and your shipment that you intend to sell on Christmas will arrive late, probably after Christmas. During this time, there is a much higher volume of shipment, which is why things get stuck at the customs.

2. Air freight

The second method of shipping is via air freight, and this is ideal if your shipment exceeds 1000 lbs. If it is below 1000 lbs, you can try express cargo, which involves a courier company such as DHL, FedEx, and UPS. However, most sellers on Amazon use either sea cargo or air freight because they usually have a lot of stuff to ship. Just like with sea freight, goods shipped via air freight also have to go through customs clearance. And just like sea freight, you also need to find a freight forwarder who will handle the entire process, including clearing customs. You have to make it clear to your freight forwarder that you want to pay for the total cost of shipping the products. You do not want to pay fees again when the shipment reaches your home or for import and export fees. This should be clarified by the freight forwarder before you decide to use their service.

Cost of air freight

When it comes to air freight shipping, the cost depends largely on the weight and volume of your shipment. Typically, air freight shippers charge per dimensional weight or actual weight, depending on which one is higher. To calculate the dimensional weight, you need to multiply the shipment's volume in CBM by 167. For example, if your shipment has a dimension of width-60 cm x height- 60 cm x length- 60 cm, you will get 216,000. Divide this by one million and you will get 0.216. To get the volumetric weight, multiply this by 167. Your shipment's volumetric weight is 36.072 kgs. If this is bigger than the shipment's actual weight, you will be charged based on the volumetric weight, or vice versa.

Compared to sea freight, air freight is a lot more expensive, especially if you are shipping heavy items. Imagine if you are shipping items that weigh a total of 2000 lbs in a medium sized box by sea from Shenzhen, China to New York, USA, you only have to pay $1200. But if you ship the same item via air freight to and from the same destination, you have to pay a whopping $4000.

Shipping time

Obviously, shipping via air freight takes a much shorter time than sea freight because airplanes are 30 times faster than ships. It will only take your shipment 3 days to one week, again depending on different factors such as speed of getting cleared at the customs, holiday season, and so on. This is why air freight is a lot more expensive than sea freight.

If you are pressed for time, you should consider choosing air freight. Maybe you are planning to sell before the holiday rush and you want your items to reach on time. Or maybe you are selling goods that have expiry dates or items that are seasonal. Electronics and other expensive items are also usually shipped via air because they will have a lower chance of getting lost or damaged because of the shorter shipping time. They are also more protected in planes than in ships in terms of storage conditions.

CO2 emissions

You already know that airplanes emit a large amount of CO_2 in the air. And if your business values sustainability, you might want to consider shipping via sea freight. According to a research conducted by the UK government, an ocean liner carrying 2 tonnes of shipment for 5000 km will only have 150 kgs of CO_2 emissions. Compare this to 6605 kgs CO_2 emissions of an airplane carrying the same load and traveling the same distance, choosing sea freight over air freight will seem like a no-brainer for people who are pro-environment and sustainability.

Import duty of products and other taxes

You also need to know the different fees involved in shipping your items. It is not just the cost of the service provided by the freight forwarder. They also have to pay different fees and taxes throughout the whole process. Import duty and taxes are calculated based on customs value and category of goods or HS code.

Customs value

Ideally, the customs value is calculated as: cost of product + cost of transportation to the Chinese port + export clearance in China. However, freight forwarders just estimate the amount at 20% to 30% of the value of the product in the United States, and this is what they declare at the customs clearance. To estimate the tariff of the product, you just multiply this amount to the current tariff rate.

HS code

Customs also assigns a standardized classification system to determine customs duty. HS Code means Harmonized Commodity Description and Coding System or simple Harmonized System. This consists of classification names and numbers to sort out traded goods that come in and go out of the country. You have to ensure that you assigned the correct HS code to your goods. Otherwise, you may be charged the incorrect customs duty.

Since you are not shipping the goods yourself, you do not really have to worry about these things because the freight forwarder or the courier company handles the entire process from start to finish. All you have to do is to be aware of these details so that you at least have an idea how much you need to pay when shipping your products. Once your products are shipped, or even before they reach their destination, you can now start preparing the products for sale by creating and building your brand.

Books In The Business and Money Series	
Series #	Book Title
1	Affiliate Marketing
2	Passive Income Ideas
3	Affiliate Marketing + Passive Income Ideas (2-in-1 Bundle)
4	Facebook Advertising
5	Dropshipping
6	Dropshipping + Facebook Advertising (2-in-1 Bundle)
7	Real Estate Investing For Beginners
8	Credit Cards and Credit Repair Secrets
9	Real Estate Investing And Credit Repair Strategies (2-in-1 Bundle)
10	Passive Income With Affiliate Marketing (2nd Edition)
11	Passive Income With Dividend Investing
12	Stock Market Investing For Beginners
13	The Simple Stock Market Investing Blueprint (2-in-1 Bundle)
14	Real Estate And Stock Market Investing Mastery (3-in-1 Bundle)
The kindle edition will be available to you for FREE when you purchase the paperback version from Amazon.com (The US Store)	

Download The Audio Versions Along With The Complementary PDF Document For FREE from

www.MichaelEzeanaka.com > My Audiobooks

Chapter 6

Preparing the Product for Sale by Branding

After receiving your items or even before receiving them, you need to prepare your products for sale by creating and building a brand. Your brand is a lot more than the name and logo of your business. It is the complete package—your products, business model, methods of advertising, values, and customer experience. This is why building a good brand is just as important as having a good product to sell.

Building a brand that is sustainable

These days, the more popular meaning of sustainability is being green and eco-friendly. And this is something that a lot of companies should strive for because more and more consumers are becoming more aware of the impact of their consumption to the environment. Another meaning of sustainability in terms of branding is lasting for a long time and remaining relevant for many years. This is also something that your business branding should aim for. You have to make sure that your branding is not just a fad or a trend. It should be sustainable and last for a long time to ensure that you have continuous business.

Choose a product that allows you to add other related products

When it comes to choosing a product to sell, you have to make sure that it allows you to add other related products as time progresses. And choose a brand that does not only focus on your specific product. For example, if you are selling quirky notebooks and your branding is something like All Quirky Notebooks, people will automatically assume that you are only selling fun notebooks with quirky designs. Sure, maybe you can add other related products like memo pads or pens and pencils, but that's about it.

What you can do is to change your branding into something more inclusive, like All Things Quirky so that you can add other related products later on as long as they have a quirky design. Another great example of this is selling electronic devices. Mobile phones, for instance, have different kinds of accessories such as cases, screen protectors, chargers, power banks, and so on. By selling complementary products, you will retain regular customers because they will not go somewhere else to look for accessories or other related products and you will also attract new customers who want to buy your other items.

Continuously create a need for your products

To keep your products' relevance in the market, you should continuously create a need for your products that will make people want to buy them. One way to do this is by promoting exclusivity of your products. For example, you can offer your products as limited editions that will make people think that they will not be sold after a particular time. You can also make your products or your promotion available only to a specific group of people. For instance, you can offer your discount or a specific product only to your Amazon customers and not to people who buy them from your physical store or other online selling platforms. This will create a need for your products that can make your business more sustainable.

What you need to know about trademarks

You always hear the word trademark but what does the word really mean? It is sometimes used interchangeably with branding which is the representation of the company. It could be a symbol, logo, phrase, or word that a company uses. Basically, a business needs a trademark to protect its intellectual property. To make your business qualified for trademark, you have to make sure that you use the brand for commercial purposes and the brand must be unique to your business.

There are certain things in your company that you can trademark such as unique names of your products and business, the words or phrases that you use for your products or marketing campaigns, symbols and logos that your company uses, and so on. You can even trademark scents, colors, and sounds that are unique to your brand and you do not want other people to use without your consent.

Types of marks

When it comes to name branding, there are four types of marks that you should know

- Descriptive,
- Suggestive,

- Arbitrary, and fanciful.

Descriptive mark is anything that has acquired a secondary meaning. For example, if you want to name your business after your last name which is McDonald's, say, McDonald's Cakes and Pastries, you will not be allowed to do so because McDonald's already acquired a secondary meaning as an American fast food chain. The most commonly used trademark is the suggestive mark. It does not entirely describe the company or the product but it gives consumers a hint of the kind of products that the company sells.

Some examples of suggestive brands are Netflix, Airbus, and Citibank. The third kind of mark is the arbitrary marking, which is a word, or phrase that has nothing to do with the company or products that they sell. One example is Apple. Apple does not sell the fruit apples but mobile phones, laptops, and computers. Windows is another great example of arbitrary trademark. Finally, fanciful marks are any original terms created for your specific business or product, such as Kodak, Aveeno, Exxon, Pepsi, and Polaroid.

Why do you need trademarks?

As mentioned before, trademarks protect your business from intellectual property theft. It also allows you to set your company and your products apart from other similar businesses to prevent confusion. Trademarks also prevent unfair competition such as imitation, trademark infringement, and use of other company's confidential information or trade secrets. Having a trademark also allows consumers to buy with confidence, knowing that the brand they are buying from is known for selling quality products.

Trademarks also allow consumers to know where the products come from in terms of the sponsor, the manufacturer, and the seller. When you apply a trademark for your business, you have to renew it after 10 years. And if you continuously use your products for five years, you can apply for incontestable status, which will give your business better rights to ownership and better protection against infringement.

Having your own trademark gives you exclusive rights to use the branding in your business. If you find other businesses using your trademark, you can pursue legal action against them because you were given the right to use that branding exclusively for your business.

Should startups register a trademark?

Some people think that trademarks are only used by large corporations such as Coca Cola or Microsoft and startups/small businesses do not really need them. This kind of thinking is the reason why some people end up losing their business. They do not anticipate these kinds of things, thinking that their business will not become as big as these corporation giants. You need to think ahead if you want your business to succeed.

It is best to protect your business from the start, especially if you have a unique branding and if your products are one-of-a-kind. This will allow you to take legal actions if your business' intellectual property rights are violated in the future. The bottom line is that you also need to trademark your brand if you want to protect your business from potential intellectual property theft in the future.

To illustrate the importance of acquiring a trademark for your brand, let's take a look at this made-up scenario. Emily started selling clothes that she designed herself in her neighborhood that she calls New Threads. She didn't bother to get a trademark for her business because she thought it was just a small business and nothing would really come out of it on a larger scale.

After some time, she noticed that a competitor in a different neighborhood who is also selling clothes also uses the same name. This case is still easy to handle because it's in a small area. As long as Emily can prove that she started using the name before her competitor, she can continue using the brand for her business.

The problem will be much more complicated if there is another competitor in a neighboring state that uses the same name and who already filed an application for a federal trademark for the name New Threads. Emily might still have the right to use the name in the area where she loves, but she can't really sell interstate because another company has already trademarked the name, which means that Emily has to change her business name if she wants to expand her business outside her town.

This could have been avoided if she filed a trademark from when she started the business. She could have chosen a different name for her business because another company is already using it. Or if she is the first one to use the name, she will have all the rights to the brand and the competitor will not be allowed to use that name in the first place. And if Emily is going to change her name to be able to sell to other states, she might lose customers because some of them might not know that it is the same company.

This is why it is best to trademark anything related to your business that could potentially cause intellectual property lawsuits and claims in the future. However, you have to make sure that you have finalized your branding before you consider filing for a trademark. Maybe in the beginning, you are still unsure about the name and logo of your business and you might still want to do some small changes to them. The most important thing to remember is to file as early as you can once you are sure about the kind of branding that you want your business to carry.

Perform a trademark search

Once you have decided to have your name or logo trademarked, the first thing that you need to do is to conduct a trademark search. You need to understand that just because your trademark application was approved, that does not mean that no other company is using it. As a business owner, it is your responsibility to find out if someone else has already used the name you chose for your business. This means that a company who owns the trademark to the name that you are both using has all the right to take a legal action against you. If the other company wins the case, you need to stop operating your business under that name.

You can do a personal search online, which is relatively easy and inexpensive. This will not be your final search but is just a preliminary search that will filter out a lot of names that have already been trademarked. You can conduct your own trademark search by going to the following websites:

- http://www.wipo.int/branddb/en/
- https://www.tmdn.org/tmview/welcome
- http://tsdr.uspto.gov/
- https://igerent.com/trademarkstudy

Aside from conducting your own trademark search, you can also seek the help of a professional. Be sure that the searches that these companies perform include not only state registered marks but also federal. And you shouldn't just be searching for registered trademarks. You also have to make sure that you also search unregistered trademarks. Although you will have a bigger chance at winning a case against a company who hasn't registered their name, you still wouldn't want to experience the hassle of proving that you own the rights to your brand.

How much does it cost to register a trademark?

You can go about this in two different ways. The first one is to file the application yourself either online or on paper. You can submit your trademark application via an online service or using TEAS or Trademark Electronic Application System. The fees for applying online can range from $225 to $400 per class of services or goods. If you decide to go via the paper route, you need to pay $600 per class of services or goods. The more types of products or services you are planning to sell under that name, the more trademark fees you have to pay. Keep in mind that the fees are non-refundable even if your application to register the trademark was rejected.

The second way to register a trademark is by hiring a lawyer. Depending on the lawyer, you may need to pay around $125 per hour or more, or a flat fee decided by the lawyer.

As stated previously, you need to renew your trademark application every ten years, which will cost you $300 if you do it online, or $400 if you submit a paper application.

Now that your products are ready, you now need to launch your products to the public. You can check out the next chapter that will talk about the step-by-step process on how to do a product launch.

Books In The Business and Money Series	
Series #	**Book Title**
1	Affiliate Marketing
2	Passive Income Ideas
3	Affiliate Marketing + Passive Income Ideas (2-in-1 Bundle)
4	Facebook Advertising
5	Dropshipping
6	Dropshipping + Facebook Advertising (2-in-1 Bundle)
7	Real Estate Investing For Beginners
8	Credit Cards and Credit Repair Secrets
9	Real Estate Investing And Credit Repair Strategies (2-in-1 Bundle)
10	Passive Income With Affiliate Marketing (2nd Edition)
11	Passive Income With Dividend Investing
12	Stock Market Investing For Beginners
13	The Simple Stock Market Investing Blueprint (2-in-1 Bundle)
14	Real Estate And Stock Market Investing Mastery (3-in-1 Bundle)
	The kindle edition will be available to you for FREE when you purchase the paperback version from Amazon.com (The US Store)

Download The Audio Versions Along With The Complementary PDF Document For FREE from

www.MichaelEzeanaka.com > My Audiobooks

Chapter 7

Product Launch

Conducting a product launch is important if you want to let people know about your products and business. A product release is different from a product launch. A product release is just a company releasing a new product and announcing it to the public. A product launch is more fun and exciting, and usually creates buzz and stirs interests among the general public. A product launch is not just something internet marketers do. Everyone who has target customers or audience can do a product launch and will benefit from it, especially startups like your business.

Reasons for doing a product launch

Create a cash windfall

For those who do not know, a cash windfall is a sudden increase of income due to a single event, such as a product launch. One popular example is Apple's product launch of their latest iPhone. Their product launch was extremely successful because people lined up to different stores all over the world to be one of the very first ones to own the new iPhone. Apple experienced a spike in sales several days after the launch of the product because they were able to create hype around their latest gadget for sale, and people participated in the hype and bought iPhones within a few days after its initial release. If your product launch is successful, you will also experience a cash windfall.

Leave a lasting impact

Although the main objective of starting a business is to earn money, you should also want to leave a lasting impact on others, especially the people who patronize your product. You can achieve this if you do a product launch. If you conduct a product launch for your goods made of bamboo, you will be known as that startup company that sells sustainable and eco-friendly products made of bamboo.

Achieve strategic positioning

Conducting a product launch also helps you properly position your business and your products in the market. There is already a lot of businesses selling things made of bamboo, so how can you position your business in such a way that you are not just another business selling bamboo products? You need to make sure that in your product launch, you position your products using the superlative—the "most affordable", the "most sustainable", etc.

Gain more customers

If you don't have a product launch for your business, only a few people will know about your business—your family, your friends, your family's friends, your friends' friends, etc. But if you have a product launch, more people will hear and know about you, even those people whom you are not connected with in any way will know about your product. And the more people know about your business and products, the higher your sales potential will be.

Establish your authority

Businesses that have product launches are most often considered the authority in the industry. This is because they are more visible to the general public. Anything that is more visible to the eyes of the public is more likely to have a bigger influence over them. And you can achieve visibility for your business by doing a product launch.

Open doors

Product launches are not only done for your intended customers. Other people who may help you with your business such as other owners of startups, influencers, manufacturers, and so on will also hear about your products. This can also help you build your network or connections that can help you get ahead in your chosen industry.

How to do a successful product launch?

Run Facebook Ads

Many successful Amazon sellers use Facebook Ads to boost their rankings on Amazon and also to increase sales, while at the same time creating a network of audience that consists of fans who cannot get enough of your products. Running Facebook Ads is one of the most cost-efficient sources of traffic outside your online selling platform, in this case, Amazon. It is no wonder because there are over 2 billion people who actively use Facebook every month. Facebook Ads are shown to people who are interested in your product or anything related to it. And these same people will most likely be converted as your buyers.

One important thing that you should do is to create a landing page. Do not make the mistake of most sellers who lead traffic directly to their Amazon products. Remember that people who are browsing on Facebook are not looking to buy anything. Besides, there is no way for you to collect your potential customers' contact information if you direct them to your Amazon listing right away. A landing page can do this for you. If you can't capture their email address and they don't buy from you, you will no longer have any way to contact them in the future to make them interested again in buying your product.

Basically, the route of a customer that comes from Facebook should look like this:

Facebook → Landing Page (capture email, send promo code) → Amazon (sale).

Split testing is also a must when it comes to running ads on Facebook. It is creating different versions of your ad based on your target audience. If you are selling clothes and you have two kinds of audience, one is a mother and the other is an unmarried female, you should use two different pictures or copy according to their different needs. A mother will most likely click on wholesome and practical pictures while a single female will be more interested in something fun and flirty. I go into a lot more details in my book Facebook Advertising – Your Step by Step Guide To Generating Quality Leads For Your Business At a Very Affordable Cost

Create a Facebook fan group

This one is quite popular. If you are an active user of Facebook, you are most likely a member of at least one Facebook group. If you live under a rock and you have no idea what a Facebook group is, it is a page on Facebook regarding a certain topic or interest where a group of people join and interact with each other. There are Facebook groups for people who love to crochet, for people who love Ariana Grande, and so on. You can also create a Facebook group for your business. This allows you to network, recruit brand ambassadors, establish relationships with customers, support customers who need assistance, and create a community for your business.

Run Amazon ads

The first step that you need to do to run Amazon ads is to create a campaign. Just select a product that you want to advertise, set a budget, and decide on the length of your campaign. For instance, you can set a $10 budget per day and not set any end date for your campaign so that Amazon users can see your ad anytime. You can either choose automatic or manual targeting that allows you to pick keywords for your products. Automatic targeting is best for beginners. Once you have completed the setup, your sponsored products will be launched immediately. Your ads will then be shown to customers who are searching for your products or related items. When they click on your sponsored product ad, they will be directed to your product listing where they can read the product details and information.

Build an email list

This is one of the key elements of modern marketing. An email list is a collection of your visitors' and customers' email addresses that you can use for marketing. You can send promotions, news, and updates about your business via email to your existing and potential customers. You cannot just randomly ask people for their email address because that will look a little scam-y. You need to use effective and subtle strategies that will make people give you their email address. One way to do this is to create a personalized CTA or call-to-action for your landing page, blogs, or any write up about your business.

A CTA is something that a visitor of the page has to do, such as "Click on this link to answer a free quiz" or something like that, and then they will be asked to enter their email address to see the results. Product launches are also a great way to get email addresses. You can ask all participants to leave their contact information to register. You can also ask them to register on your website if they want to learn more about your products. Conducting contests, raffles, and giveaways on different social media platforms or during your product launch is also a great way to build your email list.

Do giveaways

There are different ways to do a giveaway. One way to do this is by posting your giveaway event on your Facebook page or group and asking your members or followers to join by simply typing in their email address, tagging their friends, and sharing your page. This is also a way to build your email list. You can also do it by sending out details of your giveaways to your email list. There is also a lot of websites that you can use to promote your contests and giveaways for free such as the ones below:

- http://www.giveawaymonkey.com/submit-giveaway/
- https://www.theprizefinder.com/upload-competitions
- http://juliesfreebies.com/giveaway-submission-form/
- http://giveawayfrenzy.com/giveaway-submit/
- http://www.totallyfreestuff.com/submit.asp?m=13

All you need to do is to provide the details of your giveaway or contest and once they are live on these sites, you can share them on your Facebook page and group, Instagram page, blogs, and other online platforms.

Get reviews

One reason why you want to conduct a product launch is to let people know about your product and get reviews from them. Having reviews, especially positive ones, is beneficial because people are more confident to buy a product that has a lot of positive reviews. Selling great products is already a given if you want to get positive feedbacks from your customers. But to get them to review your product in the first place is the challenging part. What you can do is to send an email requesting reviews or feedbacks to your email list.

You can also ask your Facebook community to write reviews and leave a rating after using your product. Amazon also offers the Early Reviewer Program for new sellers because they know how difficult it is to obtain a review from your first time buyers. For a fee of $60 per SKU, Amazon will send an email to those who have already bought your product, offering them an incentive of up to $3 for writing a review. To be eligible, you have to be a registered seller in the U.S. and your product should cost at least $15 and up and has less than five reviews at the moment.

Choosing the right photographer for your product

For your product launch or your business in general to be successful, you need to have high quality pictures that will encourage people to buy your products. The picture should not only be clear but also accurate and honest. You may have a good DSLR camera, but if you are not a professional photographer, the pictures may still not look quite as good as what you see online. This is why it is better to hire someone who can take professional pictures of your products. You may need to pay extra but at least, your pictures will look amazing.

To choose a photographer, here are the things that you need to consider.

1. Portfolio.

Professional photographers should have a portfolio where you can see their past works and projects with different clients. You will know if their photography style suits your needs. It is best to choose a photographer who has already worked with online sellers previously because they know what needs to be done.

2. Experience.

Ideally, you should hire a photographer that has at least three years of experience taking pictures professionally. Hiring a newbie may be the cheapest option, but it can be risky because you have no idea how they work and what kind of photos they can create.

3. References.

Asking for references is a good way to know more about the photographer from a past client's perspective. You can ask about the photographer's work ethics, honesty, professionalism, and quality of output.

4. Pricing.

Be sure to ask about the pricing before you make any commitment. The pricing should be clarified in advance so that there will be no misunderstanding or surprise expenses in the future. You can either pay per image or per package deal, depending on how many pictures you need.

5. Communication.

The photographer should also be easy to contact. You might have some specific styles in mind and details that you want to highlight about the product, and these are things that you should tell the photographer. You should have the photographer's email address and phone number in case you need to ask or tell them something.

6. Free trial.

You can also ask for a free trial before you decide to hire the photographer's services. This is a great way to learn more about the photographer's creative style and work ethics.

Optimizing product listings to boost sales

If you want to improve the ranking of your Amazon listing that will make your product more visible to Amazon users, which in turn will increase your sales, you need to know how to optimize your product listing. Amazon product optimization is one of the best things that you can do for your business. There are different ways to do this.

Optimizing keywords

You already know how this works. The use of good keywords is the key to the success of your online business. Put yourself in the shoes of your target customer. If you are planning to buy, say, Disney bed sheets, you will definitely type Disney bed sheets in the search field. As a seller, you should use Disney bed sheets as your keywords. But you can also use additional keywords such as Aladdin bed sheets (or whichever Disney character you have), Disney bedding, Disney bed linen, and so on. These are the relevant keywords for the product that you are selling. If you just put bed sheet in your product listing without the word Disney, your item will not appear when a customer looking for Disney bed sheets searches for the product specifically. Here are some things that you should know when creating your listing:

- Your product title should include the top five keywords.
- You should add generic keywords (or backend keywords) aside from your most relevant keywords that do not exceed 249 bytes.
- You can use keywords in your product description and bullet lists, but make sure that the sentences still flow naturally.
- You can also add keywords (men/women) to make sure that you reach your target buyers.

Optimizing the content

Keyword optimization ensures that your product appears in the search results when the customer types relevant and related keywords. Optimizing your content, on the other hand, will make your target customer click on your listing. To improve your content, you need to focus on these three important points:

- Product information,
- Product texts and
- Images.

Product text and information overlap because they are both about the write up or description of the product. Product information is about the details that a buyer needs to know about the product such as the dimension, weight, material used, features, and so on. The advantages or benefits should also be included. The product text, on the other hand, is the way you present it to the customer. All these details and information should be presented in such a way that they are easy to read and understand. You can present some of the information in bullet points and be sure to be as straightforward and concise as possible.

The images that you use for your product listing should also be optimized. After all, this is the first thing that the customers see in the search results. You need to post one main image and additional images. The main image should show the core product as clearly as possible. It should have a white background and occupy 85% of the image frame. You can add more pictures for the accessories, packaging, demonstrative graphics, important features, environments, and so on.

Avoid duplicate content

One common mistake that online sellers make is using the same content in all their online selling platforms. Duplicate content is a big no-no because search engines will see this and think that you are copying content when both are just written by the same person—you. You should use a different write up for your Amazon listings, a different one for your own website, and so on.

Anatomy of a product listing

a) Product title

Amazon gives you a 250-character limit or about 50 words to write your product title. You need to use it wisely by making sure that all the words are important. When writing the product title, you have to keep in mind that you are writing for humans, not robots. Amazon may be using algorithms but these algorithms are still based on the search patterns and behaviors of humans. *You should also consider adding at least one key element or a benefit that sets your product apart from the products sold by your competitors*. For example, you can add keywords like biodegradable or eco-friendly. And remember that the keywords that you put in the title are more important than the words in the description because this is what the algorithm is looking into, so choose your words carefully. Make sure the keywords in your title are relevant to your product.

b) Product photos

Amazon allows you to upload up to 9 photos and you should definitely use all of them. When people scroll through the results of their searches, the first thing that they look at is the image, then the title. They will only click on the listing if they find the image and the title interesting. This is why you have to make sure that your image catches the attention of your target buyers. Your main image should have a white background and should be 85% of the entire frame. In the remaining pictures, you can show different angles of the product, zoomed parts, the packaging, and so on.

c) Important features

The character limit of this part of your listing is around 240 words or 1000 characters. It is best to write a bulleted list because no one likes reading a text heavy paragraph. You should have at least five bullets and *the most important features should be at the very top of the list.*

d) Description

This is where you can write in sentences but you should still make sure that your paragraphs are not too long. You can elaborate on the features that you already have in your bulleted list and add more important details about the product. The limit is 2000 characters including spaces, which is about 300 words.

Amazon Advertising (AA)

Amazon Advertising (formally called Amazon Marketing Services, AMS) is a system or a set of online tools that help sellers drive traffic to their listings. This was touched briefly while discussing how to run ads on Amazon and you already know that there are two types—automatic and manual. Basically, manual targeting depends a lot on you as the seller. You have to do some research and define your target keywords yourself. Automatic AA, on the other hand, is much simpler and easier because you leave everything to Amazon. All you have to do is to set it up.

Whether you are using manual or automatic, you can still get the same kinds of benefits. The first one is that you improve your visibility to potential customers by improving your ranking using relevant keywords. It also helps increase your sales at a faster rate, which makes Amazon more willing to promote your products. After all, Amazon will be more than happy to help sellers who have fast moving items.

Using AA ads search report to your advantage

Did you know that you can check how well your keywords performed in the actual searches? All you need to do is to download the data that will give you valuable insight about your keywords.

You can pull out account-level data and also choose dates that you want to study in the past 90 days. This way, you will see what makes your campaigns successful or not. For example, if you see a significant increase in sales in the past two weeks, you can pull out the data from that time frame and check out how customers reached your listings in terms of the keywords that they used. You can also determine which keywords do not work. This way, you can use the effective keywords and discard the ineffective ones in your future listings.

Testing different price points

Pricing is not as easy as adding a few dollars to the original cost to earn a profit. There are so many other factors that affect pricing and have nothing to do with how much has been spent making the product. The demand, for instance, hikes up the price. Just look at hotel rates and airfare. The price of your product also will dictate its perceived value. For instance, if you are selling a pen for a dollar, people will think it is just an ordinary pen. But if you are selling it for $100, people will think that there must be something special about that pen. And of course it should have something special about it. Maybe it is gold-plated or it was a designer pen. You cannot simply increase the price without a valid reason to do so. The price of your product gives people an idea about the quality. So be sure that your product meets their expectation.

To decide on your products' pricing point, you need to conduct a competition analysis. This means that you have to research on your competitors' prices. How much are they selling the same product? Are people buying them? This is important, especially if there is a lot of other vendors selling the same thing. It is difficult to increase your price because buyers will surely pick the cheaper option if the items are just identical.

You can either sell something unique which no one has ever sold before so that you can dictate the pricing of the product in the market. Or you can add value to your product and make it stand out. You can also do some simple manipulations such as using a different picture or name. If you find in your research that the same product that you are selling range from $5 to $10, you might want to price yours at $7. People will not go to the cheapest one because they will think there is a catch or maybe the quality is too low. They will also not buy the expensive one because they can find cheaper options. They will surely go for the mid-priced item because it meets all their needs.

You can also try split testing on Amazon. You can do this by tweaking certain parts of your listing to know which ones give you the highest sales. You can change the product title, the bullet points in your product description, the images, and of course, the price. For example, on the first couple of months, you can set the price of your pen at $1 each. The next couple of months, you can change the price at $1.50 each. After conducting your split testing, check which period gives you the highest number of sales.

When doing split testing, you should be patient because it may not tell you anything right away, especially if you are not making a lot of sales. If you only have one or two sales, you do not have enough data to work with. You should also avoid running too many tests at once because it will be hard to know what's working and what's not.

Remember that the price of the product is one of the major factors that help consumers decide what product to buy. This is why you have to choose the right pricing point for your goods.

Chapter 8

What Comes Next?

Having a successful launch does not ensure a successful business. It is just the beginning because you still have a lot of things to do. As they say, your product launch is just the beginning of your marketing journey. It's not the end goal. Pat yourself and your team (if you have one) on the back for a successful launch. Go home and enjoy your success. But afterwards, you still need to do something to maintain the success that you achieved on your product launch.

A successful product launch should touch on the first three levels of the marketing funnel.

- **Reach** - Getting your business message across to your target audience.

- **Attract** - Getting your target audience to check out your website, which will turn them into leads.

- **Convert** - Turn these leads into customers and getting them to sign up to your website and receive news and updates.

- **Educate** - Teach customers everything they need to know about your product and business to make them love your product even more.

Product launches significantly increase the volume of traffic to your website, which means that you achieve the "reach" and "attract" part of the marketing funnel. But for your launch to be considered successful, you should also have a high conversion rate, which means that people who receive your message and visit your website also sign up and buy something.

But to have consistently high sales, you need to reach the fourth stage, and that is to continuously educate your existing customers about your product to make them love your product and not buy anywhere else. You can do this by sending them news and updates about your products and ongoing promotions through email. You can also make them feel appreciated by giving them discounts and freebies.

Analyze post-launch feedbacks

A successful product launch results in people buying your products. But what about those who don't? What keeps them from buying your product? To know the answer to these questions, you need to analyze the feedbacks you receive after the launch. You probably have expectations as regards your target audience and the reasons why they are going to buy your product. These are just assumptions, which will only become clearer once you get their unfiltered feedbacks. Listen to the different feedbacks of people who buy your products and people who don't, and analyze the reasons behind their actions.

You need to analyze both quantitative and qualitative data. Quantitative data could include the number of people who give you a feedback, the number of people who participate in your launch, the number of people who give you a positive or negative feedback, the number of converted leads, and so on. Qualitative data, on the other hand, involves the content of their feedbacks. Analyze the words and phrases that they use. If the words "expensive" always comes up, it could mean that they find your products expensive which keeps them from making a purchase.

Improve the product

The act of selling a better version of a product is called upselling. To continuously satisfy your existing customers and to attract new ones, you need to make sure that your products continuously evolve for the better. To do this, you need to understand the product you are selling. What makes customers buy your products? What are the key selling features of your products? On the other hand, what are the weak spots of your product? You can find out the answers to these questions by reading customer feedbacks. To make product improvements, you can either add new features or improve existing features.

If you decide to add a new feature, be sure that it is something that will add value to your product and the customers will be happy about. Adding a new feature often creates a big marketing splash because people are excited to hear about changes to something that they already know. Outsiders will also hear about the new feature and will become curious, and might end up buying the product just out of curiosity. Adding new features may be risky, but it can also be highly rewarding if done correctly.

Improving on an existing product feature is a safer route to take, and you can do it in three different ways. The first one is deliberate improvement in which you improve on a feature so that the product works much better. The second one is frequency improvement wherein you improve a product feature so that the consumer will use it more often. And the third one is adoption improvement where the change leads to an increase in the number of people who are using the product.

Making changes on a product is a great way to maintain sales, but make sure that you are not adding unnecessary features or making unnecessary changes. Remember the saying "if it ain't broke, don't fix it"? This also applies to product improvement. This is especially true if you already have a large group of customers who have been using your product and are satisfied with it. What you can do is to create new products, which leads us to the next point.

Create new products

This is also a great way to attract more customers and make existing customers buy more. By adding new products to your already existing ones, you are reaching out to a larger group of people while at the same time not losing your loyal customers. If you simply add or improve a feature, there is a bigger chance of losing existing customers who are not happy about the change. If you simply create a new product and add it to your store, you will only attract new customers and also give more options to your existing customers. For example, if you are selling unscented shampoo bars, you can create new products with different scents and continue selling your unscented ones because these already have a loyal following. There is no reason to stop selling something that a lot of people buy.

Add complementary products

Selling new products that complement your existing products is called cross-selling. This does not mean that you are going to offer anything that you can think of. If you are selling coffee, selling teaspoons or saucers might work but it is not the perfect complement for coffee. Instead, you can sell creamer, French presses, mugs, and so on. Maybe you can sell teaspoons and saucers but only when you already have these other complementary products.

Again, put yourself in the shoes of your customer. If you buy coffee, what's the next thing that you need to buy? Teaspoons? Of course not. Creamer or sugar, maybe? Definitely. By selling complementary products, you are increasing the checkout price that the customer is going to pay even though he or she was only planning to buy coffee. With that being said, one advantage of cross-selling is increasing your sales because they buy more products from you.

Selling complementary products also improves customer loyalty. This is because your customers will feel satisfied whenever they buy from your shop because they have everything they need. It improves customer experience, which results in loyalty to your brand. Selling complementary products is also easy to manage because it is like buying a bundle. And you know that it is more cost-effective and easier to manage if one person buys two complementary products than if two people buy one same product each. This is also a great way to introduce less popular products. If you really want to sell your teaspoons and saucers, you should first sell your mugs and teacups. This way, people would want to buy the complete set. It would be weird if you're just selling teaspoons and saucers.

There are two terms that you need to know to understand the main objective of cross-selling—skimming and consumer surplus. Skimming is trying to sell a product at the highest price possible at the beginning. Later on, the price of these same products is lowered so that people who are not willing to spend the initial price can also buy the product. Skimming is basically trying to get as much money from your customer as possible. Doesn't sound too ethical, but selling products and starting a business is all about earning profits, right? Not so.

Consumer surplus, on the other hand, is the difference between the amount that a customer is able and willing to pay (depends on the demand) and the amount that they actually spent (depends on the current market price). As the demand for your product decreases, maybe it is no longer trendy or it is almost the end of the season for selling it, the price of your product will decrease. And you can no longer implement skimming because your product is no longer in demand.

Cross-selling helps minimize consumer surplus by offering them a complementary product. Let's say, a customer is willing to spend $50 on a pair of shoes which was trendy months ago, but because of the decrease in demand, you are just selling it for $30, which gives you a $20 consumer surplus. To make the customer spend this amount on your shop, you should try offering complementary products such as socks, insoles, shoelaces, running shorts and t-shirts, and so on. This way, the customer is still spending the entire $50 on your shop. You still make him spend all the money that he is willing and able to spend on your shop.

This is the reason why a lot of businesses bundle things together. Just look at fast food chains like McDonalds, which sells burgers with fries and drinks. Or gaming consoles like Nintendo, which also includes a couple of games and a controller in their bundle. They also upsell by asking you if you want to upsize your drinks and fries or by offering you a higher version of the gaming console.

The key to a successful cross-selling is anticipating your customers' needs. Again, you shouldn't just offer complementary products just for the sake of making an offer because that's just annoying. You need to know if the customer *actually* needs it.

Different ways to cross-sell

a) Sending a follow-up email

You can manually cross-sell by sending an email to your customer. For example, if a customer recently bought a laptop from your shop, you can send a follow up email after a few days offering him accessories such as a laptop bag, mouse, laptop sleeve, and so on.

b) Using a customer's browsing history

There is also automatic cross-selling which Amazon is extremely good at. If a customer visits Amazon and searches for baking sheets, even without actually buying one, your browsing history will be saved. When you visit the website again, you will see suggested products for baking such as baking molds, pans, spatula, rolling pin, and so on.

c) Social proofing

You will also see what other people bought or searched for while you are looking at a particular item. When you see that a lot of people are also buying the same items, you feel more confident about buying the same thing. It's just how humans work. We are social beings, after all, and we value our peer's approval. You will feel that your decision to buy a certain product is validated. Moreover, you will become curious when you see that certain products are bought together by some people. And you will end up buying the bundle yourself because other people are doing it, so there must be a reason.

d) Using a customer's wish list

If you have a wish list saved in your account, they will also customize the suggested products that you see based on the items that you have on your wish list. Your buying history also plays an important role on how the algorithm decides which products you may be interested in.

e) Offering minor yet essential products

You can also sell essential yet minor products to make your main product work. One great example is batteries. If you are selling battery-operated toys, you can be sure that people will also want to buy batteries for these toys. And of course they'd rather buy the batteries from the same store where they bought the toys than to search for them somewhere else. It's not much but it is still a sale.

f) Selling an entire look

Another great example of cross-selling is selling an entire outfit, for those who are selling clothes. You can make suggestions based on what goes well with a particular clothing item. It is just like having a mannequin in your online store. The mannequin gives ideas to potential buyers on how the clothes can be styled and worn. You can do the same thing by creating outfits from your products.

Believe it or not, people who are clueless when it comes to putting together an outfit always appreciate it when there is a complete outfit that they can buy without thinking too much about it. IKEA is also good at this. They showcase room designs using IKEA products and people go crazy over them. They give people ideas on how to decorate their own space using mostly IKEA furniture and décor, of course. This creates a desire among the consumers that they should get the whole look because they can see how great it looks.

When is the best time to cross-sell?

There is not one perfect time to cross-sell because it depends on the customers buying behaviors. However, you might still want to look at the different moments when customers are more willing to buy complementary products.

- You can make offers while the customer is still looking to buy the first product. This is where Amazon comes in. They customize what a buyer can see when they start browsing and shopping by suggesting products that other people bought or products that complement what the customer is planning to buy.

- You can also cross-sell in the shopping cart, just before the customer completes the transaction. This way, they can add the extra before they check out, which will instantly boost your sale for that day.

- There are people who do not want to be distracted during the entire buying process. In this case, it is best to offer them complementary products after completing the transaction, on the thank you page. Some sellers think that the thank you page is not really useful aside from telling the customer that you appreciate their business but it is actually a great page to offer more. They are in a great mood because their transaction was successfully completed and you have their trust and confidence. Plus, they still have their credit card with them so be sure to take advantage of the thank you page.

- You can also send them emails a few days after making a purchase.

- Retargeting, or indirect cross-selling through advertisements, is another great way to offer complementary products. You can use Facebook ads and ads from other platforms to make customers buy complementary products.

You do not have to choose only one method. Just choose which one to use. For instance, if you notice customers are always abandoning their carts, you should not cross-sell before they complete the transaction to prevent distractions. You can also combine two or more methods and test out different strategies at different times to see which ones work best for your business.

Explore opportunities for cross-selling

If you have no idea what to cross-sell, you might want to do a little research for you to get an idea what other products will complement the ones that you are already selling.

- The first thing to do is to check your competitors' listings and see what kind of complementary products they are offering. If you are selling shoes, check out other vendors that sell shoes and see what they offer as add-ons.

- You can also conduct a survey by sending it to your email list or by posting it in your Facebook group. Ask them what they would like to see in your store or what kinds of products would go well with your main products.

- Asking your manufacturer what complementary products they can make is also a great idea. Some people often overlook this step because they think it's all about the customers (it really is most of the time) but you should also look at the kinds of products that your manufacturer makes. This is even more helpful if they are also making products for other Amazon sellers.

Chapter 9

Scaling $10,000 a Month and Beyond

This chapter is the culmination of everything that you have learned in this e-book. Every vendor's end goal is to earn as much income as possible by selling via Amazon FBA. If you just want to help people, maybe you should just donate to charity? This is real life and in real life, you need money to pay the bills and take care of your family & loved ones. And you can earn good money by selling on Amazon. It would be even better if you can earn at least $10,000 or even more by selling on Amazon.

This is achievable because a lot of people are earning five to six figures on Amazon. How can you do that? Here are some of the important steps that have been discussed in the previous chapters and additional information that can turn your business into a money-making machine.

1. Continue evolving as a business

Coca-Cola and Apple did not reach this level of success because they have remained the same. Times change and the needs of the people and their buying behavior change as well. If your business cannot keep up with the changing times, you will surely be left behind.

A lot of people change their branding to make them look more modern. One popular example is the logo of Lord and Taylor or Instagram. They used to have logos that look old school and traditional but they changed them to make them more suitable for the modern consumers.

Another thing that you should do is to add new products, improve existing products, and add complementary products. You already know that doing these things can only lead to a significant increase in sales. Cross-selling was discussed in depth in the previous chapter, and how selling one product can lead to sales of another related product. This is why selling complementary products can improve your business.

However, keep in mind that it is best to approach this method slowly because adding too many products at the onset can be detrimental to your business. Startups should not use all their money buying different kinds of stuff to sell. It is hard to take action if your money is tied up to your inventory. It is also harder to keep track of the items that sell and the items that don't because you have way too many to track. It is also more difficult to build a core community because your customers have different interests. You can release more products once you know how your initial products did in the market.

Aside from changing your branding and adding and changing products, you should also consider adding value to your brand. For example, consumers these days are more conscious about buying things. A lot of people prefer sustainable brands which are generally lesser known than mainstream brands. This is because they promote sustainability, they are cruelty-free, they are ethical, and they are vegan. They are sometimes even more expensive than mainstream brands, but people still buy them because of this advocacy. You should also consider doing this to your brand. Make it sustainable, if you can. However, you shouldn't just do it for the sake of earning more profits. You need to do it for the right reasons for it to be successful.

2. Build an online community

These days, it is important to have an online community of people who love your products. You should never underestimate the power of social media in terms of influencing others to make decisions. These online communities such as Facebook groups and fan pages can be great support hubs for people who need help with your products. They serve as a place for updating and educating others about your business. If a new customer has a question about the product that he just bought, the community can help him by sharing their own experiences or information that they gathered from other resources. One perfect example is Amazon's Seller Central where you can discuss certain topics and issues with other sellers.

The fact that there is a community of people that joined together because of your product says a lot about your business. It means that a lot of people patronize your business and love your products, and are willing to meet others who share the same interests. These loyal customers will keep buying from you. This is why you should take care of them and make them feel appreciated. Maybe you can conduct raffles and contests for those people who are a part of your online community. Maybe you can give promo codes to those who are members of your Facebook group. Do these things and they will love you even more.

3. Continue doing product launches

If you think a product launch is only done at the start of your business, you are wrong because you can continue doing product launches as long as you have new or improved products to sell. This is why your products have to keep on evolving. You already know that doing product launches can lead to a high volume of traffic that can then be converted to sales. If you have product launches every time you have a new product or an improved feature of an existing product, just imagine how much income you will earn.

Just like what you did in your very first launch, you should also send out emails to your email list and invite people in your Facebook community to participate. The difference between your very first launch and your subsequent launches is that you now have more people in your email list and in your community. You already have loyal customers. Before, everyone was new to your product and they didn't know much about your business. You may have had achieved high traffic during your product launch, but a lot of them probably didn't end up buying. This will change when you do your succeeding launches because you now have a bigger following who know about your product and your business.

Releasing teasers leading up to the launch can also build up the hype and interest in your new product. You can maybe post a riddle about your new product days in advance. You can also conduct a countdown. Doing things like this will make the launch more exciting, and people will surely anticipate what you have in store for them. Just make sure that your product will live up to the expectation of your customers, especially since you are responsible for building up the excitement over your product.

4. Continue optimizing your product listing

Optimizing your product listing is something that you should not overlook because how your customers see your product can make or break a sale. Your product listing is the first thing that Amazon users see when they search for certain keywords in the search field. It is important that they find your listing easy to understand by presenting all the important details and information about the product as straightforwardly as possible.

If they are satisfied with the image and description, and they think that your product is what they are looking for, they will surely buy it and who knows? Maybe they will come back and buy more next time. To ensure that your product is presented as accurately as possible and that it is visible whenever an Amazon user searched for that kind of product, you need to optimize your product listing. It increases traffic to your shop, boosts sales conversion, and therefore improves profits.

The anatomy of a highly profitable product listing consists of a title, images, key product features, description, product reviews, and rating. The first four parts are the seller's responsibility and the last two come from the customers. It is not their responsibility to write a review or leave a rating, which is why you need to encourage them to do so. This will be discussed next.

5. Increase social proof

Social proof is a psychological phenomenon wherein people are more likely to do certain actions because other people are doing it as well. Knowing that someone else has already bought the product and is using it will make a consumer more confident and at ease in buying the same product for the first time. It's like people are looking for validation for their actions. In fact, study shows that product reviews are 12 times more trusted than the product description itself. You want to hear what people who have used the product have to say.

You always witness and experience social proof in your day to day life. You are more likely to eat in a restaurant filled with diners than an empty one. You have seen online clothing stores posting pictures of celebrities wearing the same clothes they are selling. People line up to buy milk tea, the latest iPhone, and so on. You think these products are worth your money because others are also buying them. Social proof is everywhere and you can also use this to your advantage.

The most important social proofing technique that you can do is to gather reviews from your customers. You can send follow up emails to customers asking them to write a review and rate the product. You can also ask your most loyal customers to create a video testimonial and post it on Amazon. Products that have more reviews are more likely to attract buyers because of social proof.

Your target should be to get 4 to 5 stars. If you have mostly 4 or 5 stars, you are on the right track. If not, you should understand why people are giving you a rating lower than 4. You need to read your bad reviews as well and do something about it. Maybe it is something that can be fixed. And gathering as much positive reviews and rating as you can will balance out a few negative reviews. As long as you only have a couple of negative reviews, you will be fine. Potential buyers will just think that the customer who gave you a bad review is difficult to please if the rest gave you positive reviews.

6. Gain more visibility using AMS

Amazon Marketing Services or AMS can help improve your product rank and your listing gain more visibility. As discussed earlier, AMS is a tool used by sellers to run ads. The ads are pay-per-click, which means that you only have to pay when an Amazon user clicks the ad. This is a great way to make your listings more visible. It is easy to set up AMS. Just login to your Amazon advertising console account and just follow the steps. When customers see your products all the time, you can be sure that your income will increase dramatically.

7. Explore creating a YouTube channel

If you want to maximize all the social media platforms, you should not forget YouTube. YouTube is a great platform for influencers and sellers because they attract huge traffic to their online stores like Amazon. For instance, a lot of resellers on online selling platforms such as eBay, Poshmark, and Depop have YouTube accounts and have hundreds of thousands of subscribers and viewers. These people may not know about their online store but after watching their YouTube videos, they will visit the store and end up buying what they have seen in the video.

Creating a YouTube channel does not only drive traffic to your online store. It can also be another source of income in itself. It is definitely a win-win situation for you because not only are you boosting your Amazon sales, you are also earning money from your YouTube videos. For instance, if you are selling clothes on Amazon, you can do a haul or a look book video using all your products for sale. People who love watching YouTube videos may see your video and love one particular outfit. They may not have bought anything from Amazon before, but they might just start now after seeing your video. If you are selling software, you can create YouTube tutorial videos. You do not really need to be in front of the camera if you are a shy person. You can ask someone to model the clothes for you or you can just simply do a voiceover and just record your tutorial on your computer.

These are the things that you can do to earn $10,000 or even more via Amazon FBA. It is definitely hard work, but everything is worth it once you start seeing the money rolling in.

Conclusion

I'd like to congratulate you for completing this book from start to finish.

I hope this book was able to help you to learn everything you need to know about selling via Amazon FBA.

The next step is to take action and do everything you have learned in this book. Come up with a product that you can sell if you haven't thought of anything yet or contact a manufacturer.

I wish you the best of luck!

Book(s) By Michael Ezeanaka

Affiliate Marketing: Learn How to Make $10,000+ Each Month On Autopilot

Are you looking for an online business that you can start today? Do you feel like no matter how hard you try - you never seem to make money online? If so, this book has you covered. If you correctly implement the strategies in this book, you can make commissions of up to $10,000 (or more) per month in extra income.

- WITHOUT creating your own products
- WITHOUT any business or management experience
- WITHOUT too much start up capital or investors
- WITHOUT dealing with customers, returns, or fulfillment
- WITHOUT building websites
- WITHOUT selling anything over the phone or in person
- WITHOUT any computer skills at all
- WITHOUT leaving the comfort of your own home

In addition, because I enrolled this book in the kindle matchbook program, **Amazon will make the kindle edition available to you for FREE** after you purchase the paperback edition from Amazon.com, saving you roughly $6.99!!

Available In Kindle, Paperback and Audio

Passive Income Ideas: 50 Ways To Make Money Online Analyzed

How many times have you started a business only to later realise it wasn't what you expected? Would you like to go into business knowing beforehand the potential of the business and what you need to do to scale it? If so, this book can help you

In Passive Income Ideas, you'll discover

- A concise, step-by-step analysis of 50 business models you can leverage to earn passive income (Including one that allows you to earn money watching TV!)
- Strategies that'll help you greatly simplify some of the business models (and in the process make them more passive!)
- What you can do to scale your earnings (regardless of which business you choose)
- Strategies you can implement to minimize the level of competition you face in each marketplace

- Myths that tend to hold people back from succeeding in their business (we debunk more than 100 such myths!)
- Well over 150 Insightful tips that'll give you an edge and help you succeed in whichever business you chose to pursue
- More than 100 frequently asked questions (with answers)
- 50 positive vitamins for the mind (in the form of inspirational quotes that'll keep you going during the tough times)
- A business scorecard that neatly summarizes, in alphabetical order, each business models score across 4 criteria i.e. simplicity, passivity, scalability and competitiveness
- ...and much much more!

What's more? Because the book is enrolled in kindle matchbook program, Amazon will make the kindle edition available to you for FREE after you purchase the paperback edition from Amazon.com, saving you roughly $6.99!!

Available In Kindle, Paperback and Audio

Work From Home: 50 Ways To Make Money Online Analyzed

This is a **2-in-1 book bundle** consisting of the below books. Amazon will make the kindle edition available to you for FREE when you purchase the print version of this bundle from Amazon.com - saving you roughly 35% from the price of the individual books.

- Passive Income Ideas – 50 Ways to Make Money Online Analyzed (Part I)
- Affiliate Marketing – Learn How to Make $10,000+ Each Month on Autopilot (Part 2)

Get this bundle at a 35% discount from Amazon.com

Available In Kindle, Paperback and Audio

Dropshipping: Discover How to Make Money Online, Build Sustainable Streams of Passive Income and Gain Financial Freedom Using The Dropshipping E-Commerce Business Model

How many times have you started a business only to later realise you had to spend a fortune to get the products manufactured, hold inventory and eventually ship the products to customers all over the globe?

Would you like to start your very own e-commerce business that gets right to making money without having to deal with all of these issues? If so, this book can help you

In this book, you'll discover:

- A simple, step-by-step explanation of what the dropshipping business is all about (Chapter 1)
- 8 reasons why you should build a dropshipping business (Chapter 2)
- Disadvantages of the dropshipping business model and what you need to look out for before making a decision (Chapter 3)
- How to start your own dropshipping business including the potential business structure to consider, how to set up a company if you're living outside the US, how much you'll need to start and sources of funding (Chapter 4)
- How the supply chain and fulfilment process works – illustrated with an example transaction (Chapter 5)
- Analysis of 3 potential sales channel for your dropshipping business - including their respective pros and cons (Chapter 6)
- How to do niche research and select winning products – including the tools you need and where to get them (Chapter 7)
- How to find reliable suppliers and manufacturers. As well as 6 things you need to look out for in fake suppliers (Chapter 8)
- How to manage multiple suppliers and the inventory they hold for you (Chapter 9)
- How to deal with security and fraud issues (Chapter 10)
- What you need to do to minimize chargebacks i.e. refund rates (**Chapter 11**)
- How to price accordingly especially when your supplier offers international shipment (Chapter 12)
- 10 beginner mistakes and how to avoid them (Chapter 13)
- 7 powerful strategies you can leverage to scale up your dropshipping business (Chapter 14)
- 15 practical tips and lessons from successful dropshippers (Chapter 15)

And much, much more!

Finally, because this book is enrolled in Kindle Matchbook Program, the **kindle edition of this book will be available to you for free** when you purchase the paperback version from Amazon.com.

If you're ready to take charge of your financial future, grab your copy of this book today! Start taking control of your life by learning how to create a stream of passive income that'll take care of you and your loved ones.

Available In Kindle, Paperback and Audio

Dropshipping and Facebook Advertising: Discover How to Make Money Online and Create Passive Income Streams With Dropshipping and Social Media Marketing

This is a **2-in-1 book bundle** consisting of the below books and split into 2 parts. Amazon will make the kindle edition available to you for FREE when you purchase the print version of this bundle from Amazon.com - **saving you roughly 25%** from the price of the individual paperbacks.

- Dropshipping – Discover How to Make Money Online, Build Sustainable Streams of Passive Income and Gain Financial Freedom Using The Dropshipping E-Commerce Business Model (Part 1)
- Facebook Advertising – Learn How to Make $10,000+ Each Month with Facebook Marketing (Part 2)

Available In Kindle, Paperback and Audio

Get this bundle at a 35% discount from Amazon.com

Real Estate Investing For Beginners: Earn Passive Income With Reits, Tax Lien Certificates, Lease, Residential & Commercial Real Estate

In this book, Amazon bestselling author, Michael Ezeanaka, provides a step-by-step analysis of 10 Real Estate business models that have the potential to earn you passive income. A quick overview of each business is presented and their liquidity, scalability, potential return on investment, passivity and simplicity are explored.

In this book, you'll discover:

- How to make money with Real Estate Investment Trusts – including an analysis of the impact of the economy on the income from REITs (Chapter 1)
- A step-by-step description of how a Real Estate Investment Groups works and how to make money with this business model (Chapter 2)
- How to become a limited partner and why stakeholders can influence the running of a Real Estate Limited Partnership even though they have no direct ownership control in it (Chapter 3)
- How to protect yourself as a general partner (Chapter 3)
- Why tax lien certificates are one of the most secure investments you can make and how to diversify your portfolio of tax lien certificates (Chapter 4)
- Strategies you can employ to earn passive income from an empty land (Chapter 5)
- Two critical factors that are currently boosting the industrial real estate market and how you can take advantage of them (Chapter 6)
- Some of the most ideal locations to set up industrial real estate properties in the US, Asia and Europe (**Chapter 6**)

- Why going for long term leases (instead of short term ones) can significantly increase you return on investment from your industrial real estate properties (Chapter 6)
- Why commercial properties can serve as an excellent hedge against inflation – including two ways you can make money with commercial properties (Chapter 7)
- How long term leases and potential 'turnover rents' can earn you significant sums of money from Retail real estate properties and why they are very sensitive to the state of the economy (**Chapter 8**)
- More than 10 zoning rights you need to be aware of when considering investing in Mixed-Use properties (**Chapter 9**)
- 100 Tips for success that will help you minimize risks and maximize returns on your real estate investments

And much, much more!

PLUS, **BONUS MATERIALS**: you can download the author's Real Estate Business Scorecard which neatly summarizes, in alphabetical order, each business model's score across those 5 criteria i.e. liquidity, scalability, potential return on investment, passivity and simplicity!

Finally, because this book is enrolled in Kindle Matchbook Program, the **kindle edition of this book will be available to you for free** when you purchase the paperback version from Amazon.com.

If you're ready to take charge of your financial future, grab your copy of This Book today!

Available In Kindle, Paperback and Audio

Credit Card And Credit Repair Secrets: Discover How To Repair Your Credit, Get A 700+ Credit Score, Access Business Startup Funding, And Travel For Free Using Reward Cards

Are you sick and tired of paying huge interests on loans due to poor credit scores? Are you frustrated with not knowing where or how to get the necessary capital you need to start your business? Would you like to get all these as well as discover how you can travel the world for FREE?

If so, you'll love Credit Card and Credit Repair Secrets.

Imagine knowing simple do-it-yourself strategies you can employ to repair your credit profile, protect it from identity theft, access very cheap and affordable funding for your business and travel the world without any out of pocket expense!

This can be your reality. You can learn how to do all these and more. Moreover, you may be surprised by how simple doing so is.

In this book, you'll discover:

- **3 Types of consumer credit (And How You Can Access Them!)**
- How To Read, Review and Understand Your Credit Report (Including a Sample Letter You Can Send To Dispute Any Inaccuracy In It)
- **How To Achieve a 700+ Credit Score (And What To Do If You Have No FICO Score)**
- How To Monitor Your Credit Score (Including the difference between hard and soft inquiries)
- **What The VantageScore Model Is, It's Purpose, And How It Differs From The FICO Score Model**
- The Factors That Impact Your Credit Rating. Including The Ones That Certainly Don't - Despite What People Say!
- **Which Is More Important: Payment History Or Credit Utilization? (The Answer May Surprise You)**
- Why You Should Always Check Your Credit Report (At least Once A Month!)
- **How Credit Cards Work (From The Business And Consumer Perspective)**
- Factors You Need To Consider When Choosing A Credit Card (Including How To Avoid A Finance Charge on Your Credit Card)
- **How To Climb The Credit Card Ladder And Unlock Reward Points**
- Which Is More Appropriate: A Personal or Business Credit Card? (Find Out!)
- **How to Protect Your Credit Card From Identity Theft**
- Sources of Fund You Can Leverage To Grow Your Business

And much, much more!

An Identity Theft Resource Center (ITRC) report shows that 1,579 data breaches exposed about 179 million identity records in 2017. Being a victim of an identity scam can cause you a lot of problems. One of the worst cases would be the downfall of your credit score. You don't have to fall victim to it.

This book gives you a simple, but incredibly effective, step-by-step process you can use to build, protect and leverage your stellar credit profile to enjoy a financially stress-free life! It's practical. It's actionable. And if you follow it closely, it'll deliver extraordinary results!

PLUS BONUS - because this book is enrolled in Kindle Matchbook Program, the **kindle edition of this book will be available to you for free** when you purchase the paperback version from Amazon.com.

If you're ready to take charge of your financial future, grab your copy of This Book today!

Available In Kindle, Paperback and Audio

Real Estate Investing And Credit Repair: Discover How To Earn Passive Income With Real Estate, Repair Your Credit, Fund Your Business, And Travel For Free Using Reward Credit Cards

This is a **2-in-1 book bundle** consisting of the below books and split into 2 parts. Amazon will make the kindle edition available to you for FREE when you purchase the print version of this bundle from Amazon.com - **saving you roughly 25%** from the price of the individual paperbacks.

- Real Estate Investing For Beginners – Earn Passive Income With Reits, Tax Lien Certificates, Lease, Residential & Commercial Real Estate (Part 1)
- Credit Card And Credit Repair Secrets – Discover How To Repair Your Credit, Get A 700+ Credit Score, Access Business Startup Funding, And Travel For Free Using Reward Cards (Part 2)

Available In Kindle, Paperback and Audio

Get this bundle at a 35% discount from Amazon.com

Passive Income With Dividend Investing: Your Step-By-Step Guide To Make Money In The Stock Market Using Dividend Stocks

Have you always wanted to put your money to work in the stock market and earn passive income with dividend stocks?

What would you be able to achieve with a step-by-step guide designed to help you grow your money, navigate the dangers in the stock market and minimize the chance of losing your capital?

Imagine not having to rely solely on a salary or a pension to survive. Imagine having the time, money and freedom to pursue things you're passionate about, whether it's gardening, hiking, reading, restoring a classic car or simply spending time with your loved ones.

This book can help you can create this lifestyle for yourself and your loved ones!

Amazon bestselling author, Michael Ezeanaka, takes you through a proven system that'll help you to build and grow a sustainable stream of passive dividend income. He'll show you, step by step, how to identify stocks to purchase, do accurate due diligence, analyze the impact of the economy on your portfolio and when to consider selling.

In this book, you'll discover:

- Why investing in dividend stocks can position you to benefit tremendously from the "Baby Boomer Boost" (Chapter 1)
- **Which certain industry sectors tend to have a higher dividend payout ratio and why? (Chapter 2)**

- How to time your stock purchase around ex-dividend dates so as to take advantage of discounted share prices (Chapter 2)
- **Why a stock that is showing growth beyond its sustainable rate may indicate some red flags. (Chapter 2)**
- 5 critical questions you need to ask in order to assess if a company's debt volume will affect your dividend payment (Chapter 3)
- **How high dividend yield strategy can result in low capital gain taxes (Chapter 4)**
- Reasons why the average lifespan of a company included in the S&P 500 plummeted from 67 years in the 1920s to just 15 years in 2015. (Chapter 5)
- **A blueprint for selecting good dividend paying stocks (Chapter 6)**
- The vital information you need to look out for when reading company financial statements (Chapter 7)
- **A strategy you can use to remove the emotion from investing, as well as, build wealth cost efficiently (Chapter 8)**
- An affordable way to diversify your portfolio if you have limited funds (Chapter 9)
- **Why you may want to think carefully before selling cyclical stocks with high P/E ratio (Chapter 10)**

And much, much more!

PLUS BONUS - because this book is enrolled in Kindle Matchbook Program, the **kindle edition of this book will be available to you for free** when you purchase the paperback version from Amazon.com.

Whether you're a student, corporate executive, entrepreneur, or stay-at-home parent, the tactics described in this book can set the stage for a financial transformation.

If you're ready to build and grow a steady stream of passive dividend income, Grab your copy of this book today!

Available In Kindle, Paperback and Audio

CPSIA information can be obtained
at www.ICGtesting.com
Printed in the USA
BVHW011742100920
588451BV00013B/473